Grammar
Step by Step

1

Helen Kalkstein Fragiadakis

Ellen Rosenfield

with Chants by Carolyn Graham

Dedicated to our families, with enormous gratitude for their patience and support, and to our students, with great appreciation for their inspiration over the years.

Published by McGraw-Hill ESL/ELT, a business unit of The McGraw-Hill Companies, Inc., 1221 Avenue of the Americas, New York, NY 10020.

7 8 9 10 QPD 10 09 08 07

ISBN-13: 978-0-07-284520-4
ISBN-10: 0-07-284520-1

ISBN-13: 978-0-07-111069-3 (ISE)
ISBN-10: 0-07-111069-0 (ISE)

Editorial director: Tina B. Carver
Executive editor: Erik Gundersen
Senior developmental editor: Mari Vargo
Director of North American marketing: Thomas P. Dare
Director of international marketing and sales: Kate Oakes
Production manager: Juanita Thompson
Cover designer: Delgado and Company, Inc.
Interior designer: Wee Design Group
Art: Artists from illustrationOnLine.com
Skills indexer: Susannah MacKay

The McGraw-Hill Companies

Acknowledgements

The authors and publisher would like to thank the following individuals who reviewed the *Grammar Step by Step* program at various stages of development and whose comments, reviews, and assistance were instrumental in helping us shape the project:

Tony Albert
Jewish Vocational Services
San Francisco, CA

Gail Barta
West Valley College
Saratoga, CA

Joan Bornheimer
New Brunswick Board of Education
New Brunswick, NJ

Gerald Lee Boyd
Northern Virginia Community College
Annandale, VA

Christine Bunn
City College of San Francisco
San Francisco, CA

Inocencia Dacumos
Serra Adult School
Richmond, CA

Renee Eliscu
Tenafly Public Schools
Tenafly, NJ

Judith Garcia
Miami-Dade Community College
Miami, FL

Greg Keech
City College of San Francisco
San Francisco, CA

Veronica McGowen
University of Central Florida
Orlando, FL

Elizabeth Minicz
William Rainey Harper College
Glendale Heights, IL

Denise Phillips
Hudson County Community College
Jersey City, NJ

Meredith Pike-Baky
Education Task Force
San Rafael, CA

Jeanette Roy
Miami-Dade County Public Schools
Miami, FL

Stephen Sloan
James Monroe High School
North Hills, CA

Colleen Weldele
Palomar College
San Marcos, CA

We worked with a fantastic team, and would like to express our gratitude to everyone. Thank you to Tina Carver and McGraw-Hill for supporting this project. To Erik Gundersen, Executive Editor, and Mari Vargo, Senior Developmental Editor, the words *thank you* cannot adequately express our appreciation for your support, creativity, and guidance. A big thank you also goes to our students, who with their insightful questions over the years have inspired us to look more closely at our native language and to teach it as clearly as possible.

Table of Contents

To the Teacher

Dear Colleagues,

As you know, our students are faced with all sorts of language input, and they depend on us to help them sort out the information that comes their way at school, at work, and in their daily lives. In the *Grammar Step by Step* series, we have divided grammatical information into digestible chunks that students can understand, and then provided practice in exercises that also help develop listening, speaking, reading, vocabulary, and writing skills.

With Book 1, we have zeroed in on ways to teach grammar clearly and systematically and isolated common areas of confusion in the beginning grammar class. We help students distinguish between, for example, the possessive, the contracted, and the plural *s*. And while we teach grammar, we teach lexical chunks of language associated with a theme or grammar point. For example, as students work on using the present tense for routine activities, they learn phrases used with *do*, *have*, *make* and *take*.

With over seventy-five years of English language teaching experience among us, we have worked to create material that not only goes step by step, but also engages students with contexts that they can relate to, and on occasion, be entertained by. Our contexts are varied, and the characters we portray reflect a wide range of backgrounds and ages. While the vocabulary we use is controlled so as not to distract from the grammar being studied, we have made an effort to use common and natural language that is essential for communication.

As our students work to learn English, we strive to keep them motivated, involved and rewarded, and to provide them with material that helps makes sense of the chaos of language. We sincerely hope that with *Grammar Step by Step*, your students will find some order in the chaos and have some fun at the same time.

Helen Kalkstein Fragiadakis   Ellen Rosenfield   Carolyn Graham

Overview of *Grammar Step by Step*

Grammar Step by Step 1 is the first in a three-level series of beginning to high intermediate books offering extensive grammar practice for young adult and adult learners. In *Grammar Step by Step*, small chunks of grammar are presented and practiced on a series of two-page spreads. While grammar presentation charts in many books present students with more new grammar than they can handle, the charts in *Grammar Step by Step* are designed to streamline the presentation of new grammar.

Each lesson in *Grammar Step by Step* features thorough practice of a grammar point, leading from controlled to open-ended activities. There are abundant opportunities for students to personalize learning through engaging speaking and writing tasks. Both lesser-trained and more experienced teachers will find the fresh and varied activity types meaningful and effective while enjoying the comfort of the accessible and predictable format.

Grammar Step by Step presents the content that experienced teachers expect to find in a grammar series, but also has a number of distinguishing features.

- **Flexible two-page lesson structure** allows teachers to select from a comprehensive array of lessons according to student and curricular needs.
- **Integrated skills approach to grammar** features initial listening activities that establish the grammar focus for reading, writing, and speaking tasks.
- **Carolyn Graham's chants** focus student attention on the oral/aural dimension of grammar learning while making classes lively and motivating.
- **Classroom-tested grammar points** target classic trouble spots like accurately using *make / take / do* and *their / there / they're*.
- **Engaging illustrations** in each lesson visually define key vocabulary, allowing teachers and students to focus on grammar learning.
- **Resource-rich Teacher's Manual** reduces teacher prep time with reproducible tests and 64 expansion activities—one for each two-page lesson!

Components

The complete *Grammar Step by Step 1* program includes the following components:

- Student Book
- Teacher's Manual with answer key, 64 reproducible expansion activities, and a review test for each group of lessons
- Audiocassette/audio CD with recordings of all listening scripts and all chants, featuring Carolyn Graham

Guide to *Grammar Step by Step*

Each streamlined two-page lesson follows a **predictable and accessible format.**

Margin notes remind students of relevant information that was introduced earlier in the text.

Clear and concise charts introduce grammar points in easily comprehensible chunks.

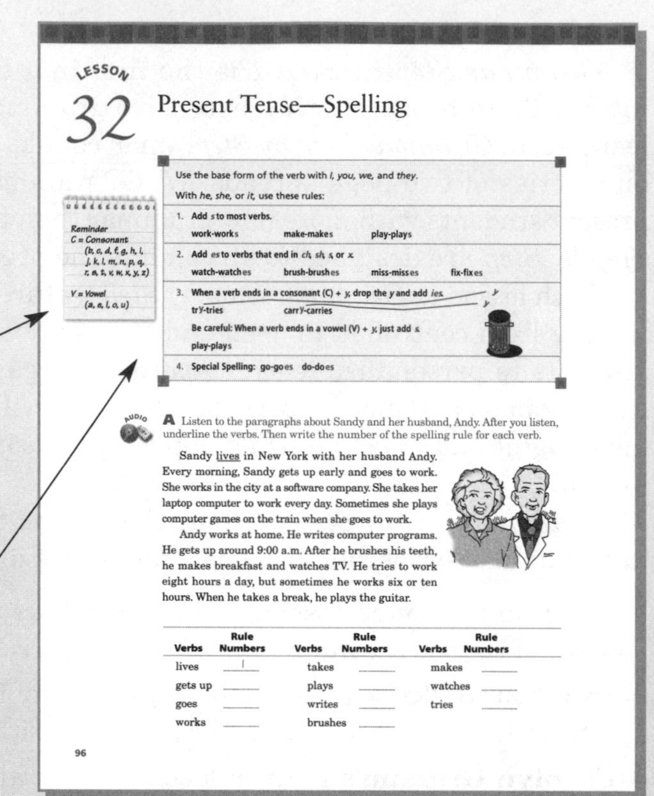

LESSON 32 Present Tense—Spelling

Use the base form of the verb with *I, you, we,* and *they.*
With *he, she,* or *it,* use these rules:

1. Add *s* to most verbs.
   work-works make-makes play-plays
2. Add *es* to verbs that end in *ch, sh, s,* or *x.*
   watch-watches brush-brushes miss-misses fix-fixes
3. When a verb ends in a consonant (C) + *y,* drop the *y* and add *ies.*
   try-tries carry-carries
   Be careful: When a verb ends in a vowel (V) + *y,* just add *s.*
   play-plays
4. Special Spelling: go-goes do-does

Reminder
C = Consonant
(b, c, d, f, g, h, l, j, k, l, m, n, p, q, r, s, t, v, w, x, y, z)
V = Vowel
(a, e, i, o, u)

AUDIO **A** Listen to the paragraphs about Sandy and her husband, Andy. After you listen, underline the verbs. Then write the number of the spelling rule for each verb.

Sandy lives in New York with her husband Andy. Every morning, Sandy gets up early and goes to work. She works in the city at a software company. She takes her laptop computer to work every day. Sometimes she plays computer games on the train when she goes to work.

Andy works at home. He writes computer programs. He gets up around 9:00 a.m. After he brushes his teeth, he makes breakfast and watches TV. He tries to work eight hours a day, but sometimes he works six or ten hours. When he takes a break, he plays the guitar.

Verbs	Rule Numbers	Verbs	Rule Numbers	Verbs	Rule Numbers
lives	1	takes		makes	
gets up		plays		watches	
goes		writes		tries	
works		brushes			

96

B Write the he/she form of the verb on the lines.

	He/She . . .
1. wake up	*wakes up*
2. get up	
3. get out of bed	
4. brush her teeth	
5. wash her face	
6. take a shower	
7. wash her hair	
8. get dressed	
9. eat breakfast	
10. drink coffee	
11. go to work	
12. take the train	
13. miss the bus	
14. stay home	
15. walk the dog	
16. make dinner	
17. study English	
18. fix computers	

get up
get dressed
take the train
miss the bus
walk the dog
fix computers

C Work with a partner. Ask your partner the questions below and take notes. Then, on a separate piece of paper, write sentences about your partner and share them with the class.

EXAMPLE: Note—*7:00*
Sentence—*Yolanda gets up at 7:00.*

My partner: ____________
(your partner's first name)

Questions	Notes
1. What time do you get up?	
2. What do you do first?	
3. What do you do after that?	
4. What do you do next?	
5. Then what do you do?	
6. What do you do after that?	

97

New vocabulary words are taught through **engaging illustrations**.

Tightly controlled exercises at the start of each lesson allow students to focus on the structure of the new grammar point.

Open-ended activities or chants at the close of each lesson provide students with opportunities to personalize the grammar point or interact with the grammar in an engaging way.

Classroom-tested grammar points target classic trouble spots like accurately using *do/have/make/take* and *their/there/they're*

The opening activity of each lesson acquaints students with the grammar point through a **context-building listening activity**.

Audiocassettes and audio CDs contain at least one listening activity per lesson, as well as 30 original chants written and recorded by Carolyn Graham.

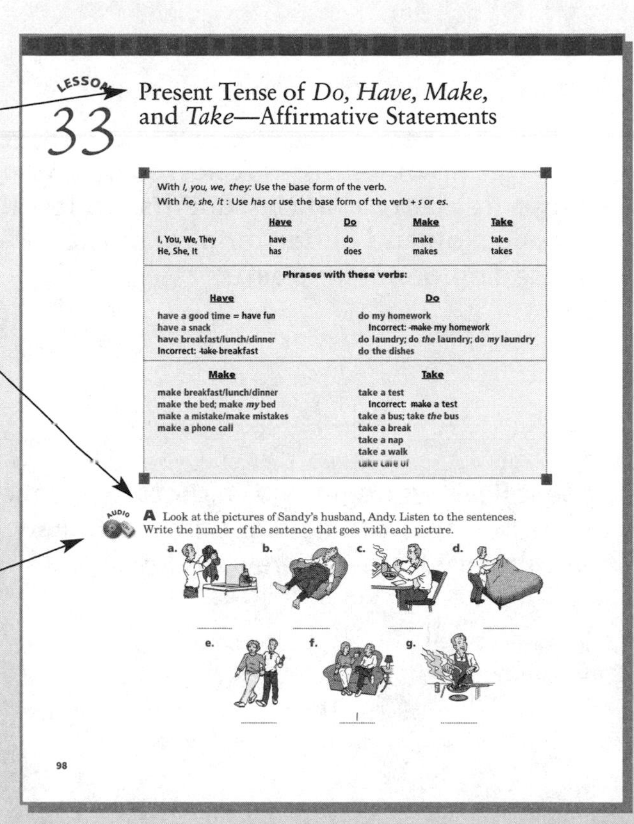

LESSON 33

Present Tense of *Do*, *Have*, *Make*, and *Take*—Affirmative Statements

With *I, you, we, they:* Use the base form of the verb.
With *he, she, it* : Use *has* or use the base form of the verb + *s* or *es*.

	Have	Do	Make	Take
I, You, We, They	have	do	make	take
He, She, It	has	does	makes	takes

Phrases with these verbs:

Have
have a good time = have fun
have a snack
have breakfast/lunch/dinner
Incorrect: ~~take~~ breakfast

Do
do my homework
Incorrect: ~~make~~ my homework
do laundry; do *the* laundry; do *my* laundry
do the dishes

Make
make breakfast/lunch/dinner
make the bed; make *my* bed
make a mistake/make mistakes
make a phone call

Take
take a test
Incorrect: make a test
take a bus; take *the* bus
take a break
take a nap
take a walk
take care of

AUDIO **A** Look at the pictures of Sandy's husband, Andy. Listen to the sentences. Write the number of the sentence that goes with each picture.

a. ____ b. ____ c. ____ d. ____
e. ____ f. ____ g. ____

98

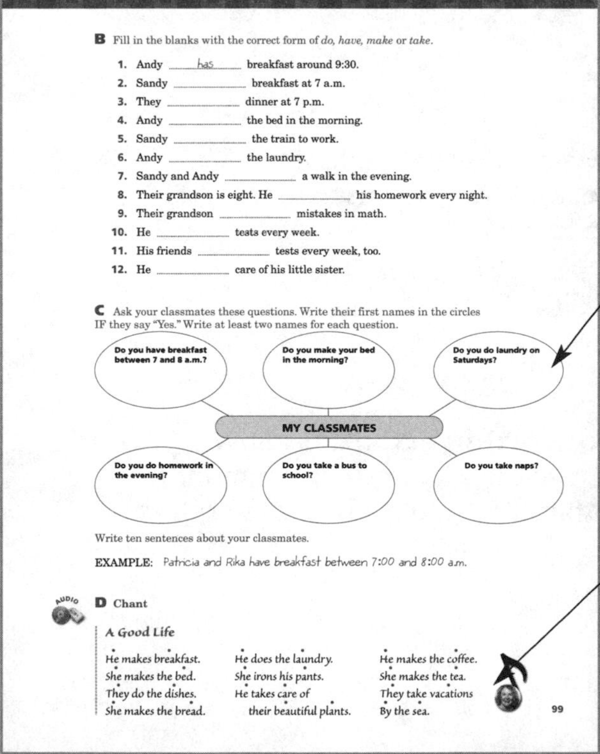

B Fill in the blanks with the correct form of *do, have, make* or *take*.

1. Andy ___has___ breakfast around 9:30.
2. Sandy ________ breakfast at 7 a.m.
3. They ________ dinner at 7 p.m.
4. Andy ________ the bed in the morning.
5. Sandy ________ the train to work.
6. Andy ________ the laundry.
7. Sandy and Andy ________ a walk in the evening.
8. Their grandson is eight. He ________ his homework every night.
9. Their grandson ________ mistakes in math.
10. He ________ teats every week.
11. His friends ________ tests every week, too.
12. He ________ care of his little sister.

C Ask your classmates these questions. Write their first names in the circles IF they say "Yes." Write at least two names for each question.

MY CLASSMATES
Do you have breakfast between 7 and 8 a.m.?
Do you make your bed in the morning?
Do you do laundry on Saturdays?
Do you do homework in the evening?
Do you take a bus to school?
Do you take naps?

Write ten sentences about your classmates.

EXAMPLE: Patricia and Rika have breakfast between 7:00 and 8:00 a.m.

AUDIO **D** Chant

A Good Life

He makes breakfast.
She makes the bed.
They do the dishes.
She makes the bread.

He does the laundry.
She irons his pants.
He takes care of
their beautiful plants.

He makes the coffee.
She makes the tea.
They take vacations
By the sea.

99

Many activities encourage students to use the new grammar point to **interact with classmates**.

One lesson in each group ends with a **chant** which allows students to practice the **pronunciation, rhythm, and intonation** of the new grammar point.

Each group of lessons is followed by a **two-page *Review*** in which students can test their recollection and understanding of the preceding grammar points.

Most Reviews begin with a **dictation** which incorporates both new grammar and new vocabulary from the previous lessons.

Lessons 31–34

Review
Present Tense

AUDIO

A Dictation Listen to the sentences about a lazy teenager. Write what you hear. Key words: *lazy, laundry.*

1. Sometimes ______
2. ______
3. ______
4. ______
5. ______

B These verbs have different *s* forms. Put the verbs in the correct list in the chart.

brush	go	play	wake	carry	try
~~get~~	stay	walk	do	make	work
study	wash	fix	miss	take	watch

-s	-es	-ies
gets		

C Use some of the verbs from Exercise B in these sentences. You can use the verbs more than once.

1. Every morning, my brother __washes__ his face, ______ his teeth, and ______ dressed.
2. He ______ the bus to school. Sometimes he ______ up late, and he ______ the bus.
3. He ______ hard at school. After school, he ______ soccer.

102

4. When he ______ home, he ______ the dog and ______ the guitar.
5. After dinner, he ______ his homework.
6. He ______ a shower at 9:00 p.m. and he ______ to bed at 10:00 pm.

D Complete the chart.

		Singular	Plural
1.	Affirmative:	He plays soccer.	They play soccer.
	Negative:	He doesn't play soccer.	They don't play soccer.
2.	Affirmative:	She goes to school.	We ______
	Negative:	She ______	We ______
3.	Affirmative:	She ______	They study English.
	Negative:	She ______	They ______
4.	Affirmative:	He ______	We ______
	Negative:	He doesn't do the laundry.	We ______
5.	Affirmative:	She ______	They ______
	Negative:	She ______	They don't have breakfast.

E Find the mistakes. Rewrite the sentences.

1. I no have a job. __I don't have a job.__
2. This class have many students. ______
3. My friend no like this city. ______
4. My husband work in New York. ______
5. I'm call my family every week. ______
6. My country have beautiful weather. ______
7. He studys hard. ______
8. He washs the dishes. ______
9. He plaies soccer. ______
10. I make my homework every day. ______
11. We make a test every Friday. ______

103

Review activities ask students to **synthesize the grammar** that they've learned.

Error-correction activities allow students to identify and fix common errors that they might make themselves.

The *Have Fun* **activities** following each group of lessons reward students for their hard work.

Puzzles, word games, and cooperative activities allow students to use the new grammar in fun and entertaining ways.

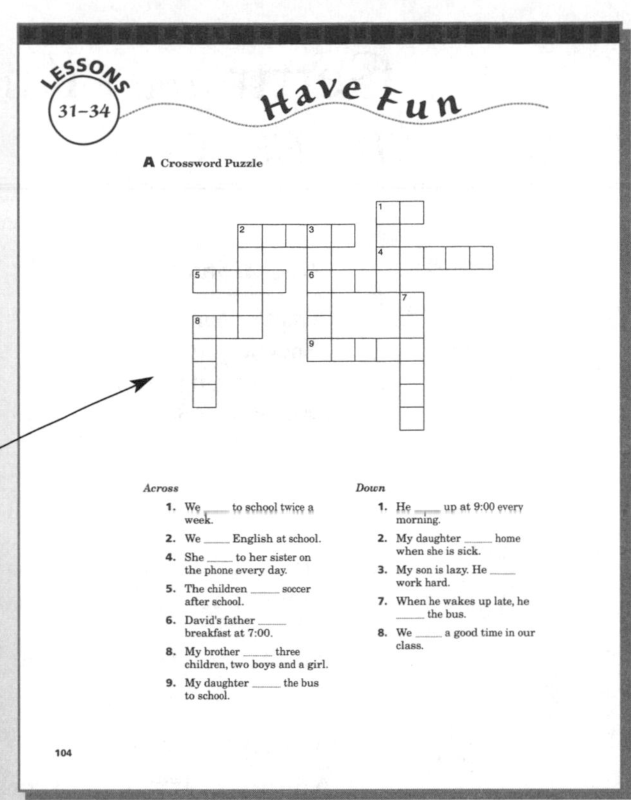

LESSONS 31–34

Have Fun

A Crossword Puzzle

Across

1. We ____ to school twice a week.
2. We ____ English at school.
4. She ____ to her sister on the phone every day.
5. The children ____ soccer after school.
6. David's father ____ breakfast at 7:00.
8. My brother ____ three children, two boys and a girl.
9. My daughter ____ the bus to school.

Down

1. He ____ up at 9:00 every morning.
2. My daughter ____ home when she is sick.
3. My son is lazy. He ____ work hard.
7. When he wakes up late, he ____ the bus.
8. We ____ a good time in our class.

104

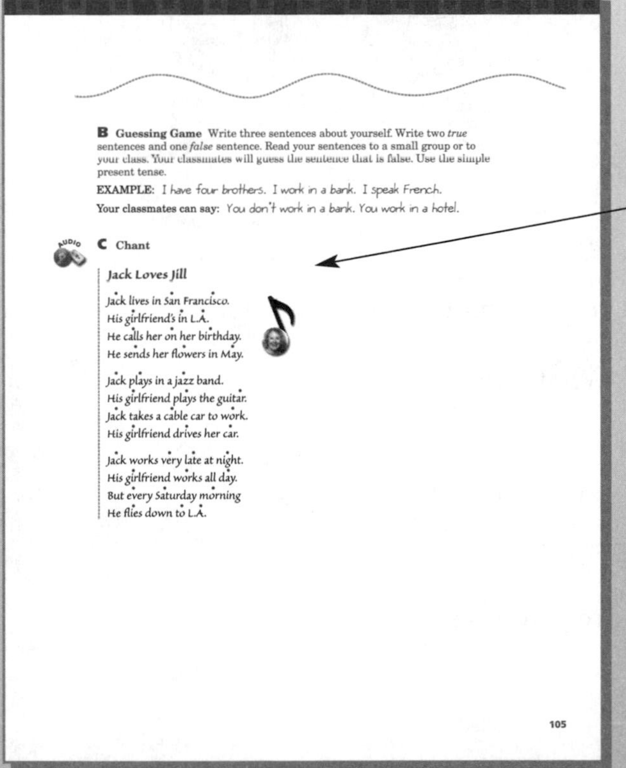

B **Guessing Game** Write three sentences about yourself. Write two *true* sentences and one *false* sentence. Read your sentences to a small group or to your class. Your classmates will guess the sentence that is false. Use the simple present tense.

EXAMPLE: *I have four brothers. I work in a bank. I speak French.*

Your classmates can say: *You don't work in a bank. You work in a hotel.*

C **Chant**

Jack Loves Jill

Jack lives in San Francisco.
His girlfriend's in L.A.
He calls her on her birthday.
He sends her flowers in May.

Jack plays in a jazz band.
His girlfriend plays the guitar.
Jack takes a cable car to work.
His girlfriend drives her car.

Jack works very late at night.
His girlfriend works all day.
But every Saturday morning
He flies down to L.A.

105

Each *Have Fun* spread closes with a lively **chant by Carolyn Graham**.

The **resource-rich Teacher's Manual** reduces teacher prep time with reproducible tests and 64 expansion activities—one for each two-page lesson!

Getting to Know You

The First Class

Questions	Answers
What's your name?	Helen./My name is Helen.
How do you spell it?	H-e-l-e-n.
How do you pronounce it?	Hé-len.
Where are you from?	New York./I'm from New York.

A Anna and Soo Jin are in English class. It is the first day of school. Listen to the conversation. Practice the conversation with a partner.

Anna: Hi. I'm Anna. What's your name?
Soo Jin: Soo Jin.
Anna: It's nice to meet you, Soo Jin.
Soo Jin: Nice to meet you, too, Anna. Where are you from?
Anna: Mexico. Where are you from?
Soo Jin: I'm from Korea.

B Complete the conversation with your partner. Then practice it.

A: Hi, I'm .... What's your name?
B: ....
A: It's nice to meet you, ...
B: Nice to meet you, too, ...
Where are you from?
A: .... Where are you from?
B: I'm from ....

C Listen to the letters of the alphabet. Repeat.

Aa	Bb	Cc	Dd	
Ee	Ff	Gg		
Hh	Ii	Jj	Kk	
Ll	Mm	Nn	Oo	Pp
Qq	Rr	Ss		
Tt	Uu	Vv		
Ww	Xx	Yy	Zz	

D Talk to a classmate.

A: What's your name?
B: My name is . . .
A: How do you spell it?
B: It's . . .
A: How do you pronounce it?
B: It's . . .

E Ask your teacher and five classmates some questions. Complete the chart.

EXAMPLE: A: Hi. What's your name?
B: Chang.
A: How do you spell it?
B: C-h-a-n-g.
A: Where are you from?
B: China.
A: It's nice to meet you.
B: Nice to meet you, too.

	First Name	Native Country
EXAMPLE:	Chang	China

Introduction

Words to Know	
1. a partner	you a partner
2. a group	a group
3. a question	What is your name?
4. an answer (a response)	My name is Helen.
5. a sentence	My name is Helen.
6. a paragraph	My name is Helen. I am from New York. Now I live in California. I am a teacher. I like teaching and writing books.
7. capital (upper case) letters	I am from New York.
8. small (lower case) letters	I am from the U.S.
9. vowels	Aa, Ee, Ii, Oo, Uu
10. consonants	Bb, Cc, Dd, Ff, Gg, Hh, Jj, Kk, Ll, Mm, Nn Pp, Qq, Rr, Ss, Tt, Vv, Ww, Xx, Yy, Zz

Directions	Example	
1. Circle.	(teacher)	
2. Underline.	teacher	
3. Fill in the blank.	I am from New York.	
4. Match.	b 1. go to	a. home
	a 2. go	b. New York
5. Write the answer on the line.	A: Where are you from?	
	B: New York .	
6. Correct the grammar.	I am ~~come~~ from New York. I am from New York.	
7. Complete the sentence.	Now I live in California .	
8. Complete the chart.	Singular	Plural
	book	books
	boy	boys
	girl	girls
9. Check the correct answer.	...... This is a books.	✔ This is a book.

A Read the paragraph. Underline the capital letters. Circle the periods. Compare your answers with a partner.

My name is Helen. I am from New York. Now I live in California. I am a teacher. I like teaching and writing books.

B Complete the chart.

	Vowels	Consonants
1.	a	b, ...c... , d
2.	....	.... , ...g... , ...
3.	....	j, k, l, ... , ... ,
4.	o	.... , q, r, s, t
5.	....	v, ... , x, ...y... , z

C Complete the sentences.

1. My ....name......... is ....

2. I .... from ....

D Check the correct answers.

1.	Vowels:	✔ a	.... z	.... D	.... u
2.	Consonants:	 I	.... f	.... m	.... E
3.	Vowels:	.... T	.... e	.... f	.... N
4.	Consonants:	.... Z	.... o	.... q	.... A
5.	Vowels:	.... F	 i	.... U	.... p
6.	Consonants:	.... O	.... G	 c	 I

LESSON

1 Nouns

Nouns are people, places, and things.

People		Places		Things	
Singular	Plural	Singular	Plural	Singular	Plural
a girl	girls	an elevator	elevators	a bed	beds

Language Notes

A or *An* with Singular Nouns

- *A* and *an* = one. Use *a* and *an* with singular nouns.
- Use *a* when the noun starts with a consonant sound (a girl).
- Use *an* when the noun starts with a vowel sound (an elevator).
- Don't use *a* and *an* with plural nouns (Incorrect: ~~a girls~~).

***S* with Plural Nouns**

- Put *s* at the end of most nouns to make them plural.

A Circle the singular nouns. Underline the plural nouns. Then listen and check your answers.

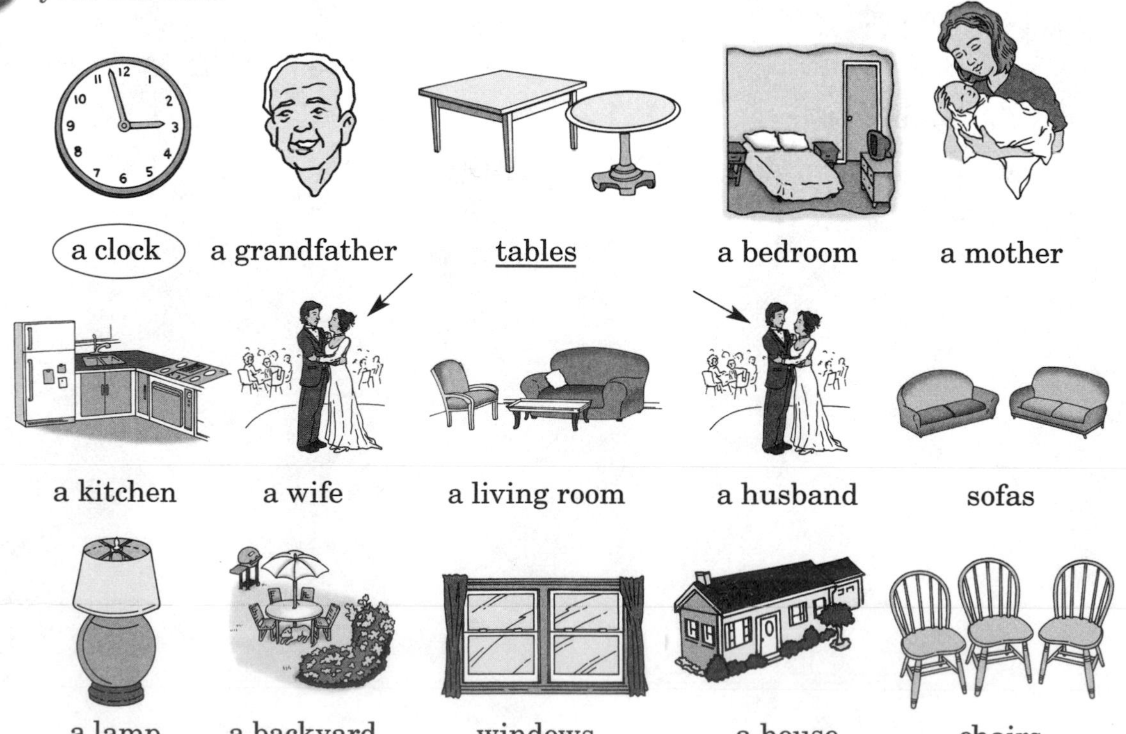

a clock · a grandfather · tables · a bedroom · a mother

a kitchen · a wife · a living room · a husband · sofas

a lamp · a backyard · windows · a house · chairs

B Now make three lists. Write the nouns in Exercise A on the lines.

People	Places	Things
a grandfather	a bedroom	a clock
....	....	....
....	....	....
....	....	....
	....	....
		....

C Check (✔) the people, places, and things in your house or apartment. You can make the nouns plural. Write more nouns on the lines.

EXAMPLE: ✔ ~~a~~ clocks

✔ a sofa

People	Places	Things
...... a mother	...... a kitchen	...... a clock
...... a father	...... a living room	...... a sofa
...... a sister	...... a dining room	...... a table
....	....	....
....	....	....

D Chant

Chairs

A room A lamp (clap)
A clock A dining room
A table A sofa (clap)
Chairs A living room
A room A window (clap)
A clock An apartment (clap)
A table Chairs (clap)
Chairs Chairs (clap)

LESSON 2

Proper Nouns and Subject Pronouns

Proper nouns are NAMES of people, places, and things.
Proper nouns start with capital letters.

People	Places	Things
Michael, Elizabeth	the United States	Coca-Cola™
	New York	Star Wars™
	Korea	Time Magazine™
	the Empire State Building	Adidas™

Subject Pronouns:

Singular	Plural
 I	we 
 you*	you* 
 he	they 
 she	
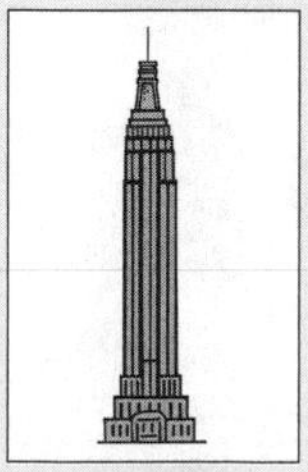 it	

*Use *you* for singular and plural.

A Listen to the pronunciation of names and nicknames. Think of some names you know. Write more names on the lines.

Male		Female	
Michael (Mike)	Robert (Rob, Bob)	Julia (Julie)	Jennifer (Jen, Jenny)
William (Bill)	Jonathan (Jon)	Anna	Katherine (Kathy)
Alexander (Alex)	....	Jessica	....
David (Dave)	....	Rebecca (Becky)	....
James (Jim, Jimmy)	....	Nicole	....

B Read the names of these places. Write more places on the lines.

Cities	Countries	Famous Places
Seoul	China	The Eiffel Tower
Paris	Vietnam	Buckingham Palace
London	Brazil	Mount Fuji
....	....	....
....	....	....
....	....	....

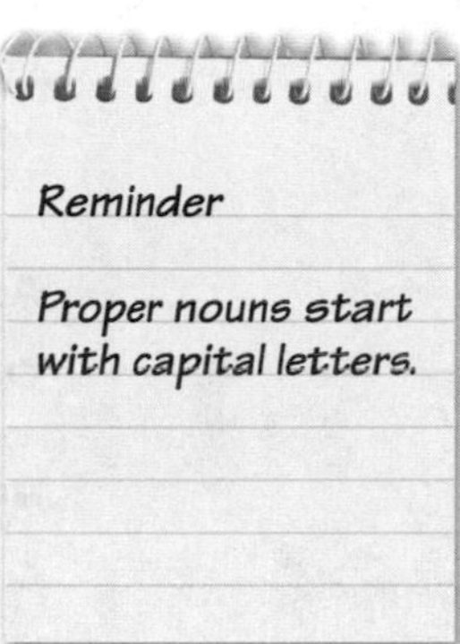

C Write subject pronouns on the lines.

1. Jonathan ......he......
2.  ....
3. David and I ....
4. David and Sara ....
5.  ....
6. Los Angeles ....
7. Elizabeth ....
8. Daniel ....
9. Disneyland ....
10. ....

D Complete the chart. Talk to two classmates.

	What is your first name? How do you spell it?	Do you have a nickname? How do spell that?	Where are you from? How do you spell it?
EXAMPLE:	Elizabeth	Liz	Texas
1.	....	....	....
2.	....	....	....

LESSON

3 Adjectives

Adjectives are words that describe nouns.

Adjectives describe people:	**a happy baby, an old man, tall girls**
Adjectives describe places:	**a clean kitchen, an old house, big apartments**
Adjectives describe things:	**a small table, an expensive car, sad movies**

Language Notes
Use *an* when the next word starts with a vowel.
- **an apartment (*an* + singular noun that starts with a vowel)**
- **an old man (*an* + adjective that starts with a vowel + a singular noun)**

Adjectives come before nouns.

Correct: a happy baby **Incorrect:** ~~a baby happy~~

Adjectives have no plural form.

Correct: big stores **Incorrect:** ~~bigs~~ stores

A Match the opposites. Listen to check your answers.

b **1.**  happy

a. 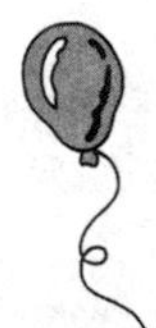 little (small)

...... **2.**  cold

~~**b.**~~  sad

...... **3.** 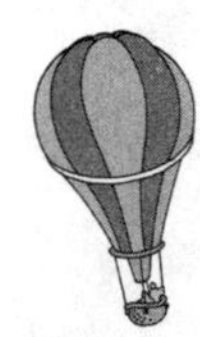 big (large)

c.  hot

...... **4.**  old

d.  young

B Match the opposites. Listen to check your answers.

.... 1.	expensive		a.	cheap
.... 2.	black		b.	short
.... 3.	long		c.	ugly
.... 4.	beautiful		d.	white

C Complete the chart with nouns (people, places, things) that these adjectives can describe. First, write what *you* think. Second, ask two students: "What is .... ?"
adjective

EXAMPLE: You: What is expensive?
Student 1: A restaurant.
You: What is expensive?
Student 2: Jeans.

Adjective	(You) Noun	(Student 1) Noun	(Student 2) Noun
1. expensive	a car	a restaurant	jeans
2. cheap			
3. young			
4. beautiful			
5. hot			
6. black			

LESSON 4

Verbs

Verbs are words that can show actions.
walk
run
talk
laugh
cook
wash
cry
dance
Verbs are also words that can show what is in our heads and hearts.
think
love
like
want

AUDIO

A Circle the word that is *not* a verb. Listen to hear the verbs.

1.	eat	kitchen	cook	wash
2.	expensive	be	pay	cry
3.	read	write	desk	listen
4.	teach	study	classroom	learn
5.	smile	dance	talk	happy

B Circle the things you do. Then work with a partner and add two verbs to each list. Use your dictionary.

For Exercise	In the House	For Fun
run	cook	play (cards)
walk	clean	go (to a party)
swim	sleep	dance
....	....	....
....	....	....

At School	In the Store	On Your Birthday
write	shop	....
read	look	....
talk	walk	....
....	....	....
....	....	....

C Fill in the calendar with things that you do. Use verbs from Exercise B. Then complete the sentences. Get into a group of four and share your sentences.

On Mondays	On Tuesdays	On Wednesdays	On Thursdays	On Fridays	On Saturdays	On Sundays

EXAMPLE: On Mondays, *I clean my room.*

1. On Mondays, I ....
2. On Tuesdays, I ....
3. On Wednesdays, I ....
4. On Thursdays, I ....
5. On Fridays, I ....
6. On Saturdays, I ....
7. On Sundays, I ....

Lessons 1–4

Review

Nouns, Adjectives, and Verbs

A Welcome to the Rodriguez family kitchen. Look at the picture and answer the questions.

1. What do you see? Write the nouns. Use *a* or *an*.

People a father ....

Things a table ....

2. Describe the people in the family. Use three adjectives. Use *a* or *an*.

EXAMPLE: a young boy

.... baby .... father .... mother

3. Describe things in the kitchen. Use three adjectives.

EXAMPLE: a large table

....

4. What actions do you see in the picture? Circle the verbs.

hold talk listen wash cook

read run cry smile drink

write sit stand eat sleep

B Bring a picture from a magazine to class. Talk about the picture in a group.

1. Write the nouns you see.

People		**Things**	
....	....	....	....
....	....	....	....
....	....	....	....

2. Describe three of the people or things in the picture. Use three adjectives.

....

3. What actions do you see? Write three verbs.

....

C Write down some people and things from Exercises A and B. Then write the subject pronoun *(he, she, it,* or *they)* on the line at the right.

	People		**Things**	
1.	father	he	table	it
2.				
3.				
4.				
5.				
6.				

LESSONS 1–4

Have Fun

A Work with a partner. Unscramble the words.

1.	N U S T E D T	S T U D E N T
2.	R C H T A E E	T E _ _ _ _ R
3.	Y U S T D	S _ _ _ Y
4.	Y A H P P	_ A P _ _
5.	N R U	_ _ N
6.	P C A H E	C _ _ A _
7.	G I B	_ I _
8.	B E T A L	T _ _ _ E
9.	W K L A	_ _ L _

B Look at the pictures of the girl. Remember what nouns, verbs, and adjectives are. Then put the words from Exercise A into the chart.

Noun: girl

Verb: laugh

Adjective: pretty

	Nouns	Verbs	Adjectives
1.	student		
2.			
3.			

C Chant

Drive, Walk, Listen, Talk

Drive, walk
Listen, talk
Drive, walk
Listen, talk

He likes to drive.
She likes to walk.
He loves to listen.
She loves to talk.

Drive, walk
Listen, talk
Drive, walk
Listen, talk

I like to listen.
You like to talk.
We like to drive.
They like to walk.

Drive, walk
Listen, talk
Drive, walk
Listen, talk

I

you

he

she

we

they

walk

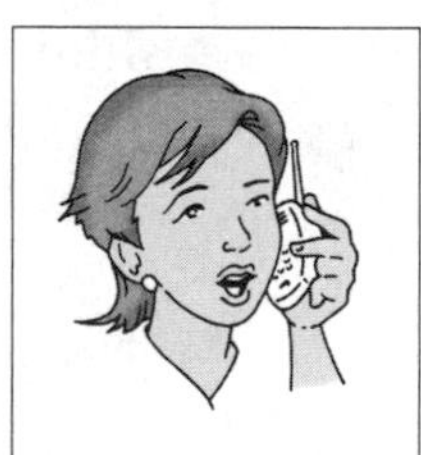

talk

LESSON

5 *BE*—Affirmative Statements

Subject Pronouns and Contractions

BE in the present tense has three forms: *am, is,* and *are.*

Full Form	Contractions
I am	I'm
You are	You're
He is	He's
She is	She's
It is	It's
We are	We're
They are	They're

A Read about these people. Underline the verb *BE* (*am, is, are*). Then listen. Practice saying the sentences with a partner.

1.

Juan is a college student. He's very busy. He's at school every day.

2.

Paul and I are twins. We're 16 years old. We're high school students. I'm a basketball player. My brother is a soccer player.

3.

Patricia is a waitress in a big restaurant. She's tired. Peter is a waiter. He's happy.

4.

Phuong is an architect. She's the boss in her office. Her office is beautiful. It's in a tall building.

B Fill in the blanks with *am, is,* or *are.*

Hi! My name ____is____ George. I ________ an English teacher. I ________ from the United States. Gabriela ________ my wife. She ________ an English teacher, too. We ________ happy together.

Hello! My name ________ Gabriela. George ________ my husband. We ________ married and we ________ teachers. We ________ from different countries. I ________ from Argentina, and George ________ from thc United States.

C Complete the chart. Write contractions.

	People say:	When you talk about the people, you say:
1.	I'm a doctor.	He's a doctor.
2.	We________ students.	They________
3.	I________ an architect.	She________
4.	I________ a waiter.	He________
5.	I________ a waitress.	She________
6.	I________ a teacher.	You________

D Complete this conversation with a partner.

A: What do you do?

B: I'm a ________. How about you?

A: I'm a ________(too).

B: That's interesting.

BE—Negative Statements

Subject Pronouns, Adjectives, and Contractions

Affirmative	Negative		
Full Forms	**Full Forms**	**Contractions**	
I am	I am not	I'm not	
You are	You are not	You're not OR	You aren't
He is She is It is	He is not She is not It is not	He's not OR She's not OR It's not OR	He isn't She isn't It isn't
We are They are	We are not They are not	We're not OR They're not OR	We aren't They aren't

A Listen. Check (✔) the sentence you hear.

1. ______ a. They're not happy.
   __✔__ b. They aren't happy.
   ______ c. They are happy.

2. ______ a. You aren't old.
   ______ b. You're old.
   ______ c. You're not old.

3. ______ a. He isn't tall.
   ______ b. He's tall.
   ______ c. He's not tall.

4. ______ a. It's cold.
   ______ b. It isn't cold.
   ______ c. It's not cold.

5. ______ a. It's blue.
   ______ b. It isn't blue.
   ______ c. It's not blue.

6. ______ a. She's not sad.
   ______ b. She's sad.
   ______ c. She isn't sad.

7. ______ a. We aren't short.
   ______ b. We're not short.
   ______ c. We're short.

8. ______ a. I'm not young.
   ______ b. I am young.
   ______ c. I'm young.

B David and Kathy are married. They are very happy. But sometimes they disagree. Write negative sentences with contractions.

1. David: This food is bad.

   Kathy: It's not bad ! It's delicious.

   It isn't bad ! It's delicious.

2. Kathy: I'm late.

   David: .... ! You're early.

   .... ! You're early.

3. David: This painting is beautiful.

   Kathy: .... ! It's ugly!

   .... ! It's ugly!

4. Kathy: You're tall.

   David: .... ! I'm short.

C Read the sentences. Write negative sentences with the same meaning. Use subject pronouns.

1. David and I are married. We aren't single.
2. David and Kathy are married. ....
3. My friend and I are young. ....
4. Kathy is early. ....
5. My brother and sister are tall. ....
6. You're fast. ....

AUDIO

D Chant

It's hot today. It's not cold.

It's hot today.
It's not cold.

She's very young.
She's not old.

He's happy today.
He isn't sad.

The students are good.
They aren't bad.

The song is short.
It's not long.

The teacher is right.
She's not wrong.

LESSON 7

BE with Adjectives and Nouns

Regular and Irregular Plurals

Use *BE* with adjectives and nouns.

Noun/Subject Pronoun + *BE* (*not*) + Adjective		Subject Pronoun + *BE* (*not*) + Adjective + Noun
The salesperson is busy.	He's busy.	He's a busy salesperson.
The waitress is tired.	She's tired.	She's a tired waitress.
The store isn't expensive.	It isn't expensive.	It isn't an expensive store.
The children aren't quiet.	They're not quiet.	They're not quiet children.

Incorrect: The mall ~~it~~ is big. The waitress ~~she~~ is tired.

Language Notes

Some nouns have IRREGULAR plural forms.

Singular	Plural (Don't add an *s*.)	Incorrect
a child	children	children~~s~~
a person	people	people~~s~~
a salesperson	salespeople	salespeople~~s~~

A Brian and Annie's family is at the mall. Read the sentences. Write new sentences on the lines. Remember to use contractions and *a* or *an*. Listen to check your answers.

Reminder

Use a or an only with singular nouns.

1. The jewelry store is expensive. It's an expensive jewelry store.
2. The bookstore is crowded. It ________.
3. The music store is noisy. It ________.
4. The salespeople are friendly. They ________.
5. The children are happy. They ________.
6. The restaurant is great. It ________.
7. The waitress is young. She ________.
8. The waiter is old. He ________.

B Make the sentences from Exercise A negative. Write each sentence in two ways—with an adjective only and with an adjective + a noun.

	Noun + *BE* + *not* + Adjective	Subject Pronoun + *BE* + *not* + Adjective + Noun
1.	The jewelry store isn't expensive.	It isn't an expensive jewelry store.
2.		
3.		
4.		
5.		
6.		
7.		
8.		

C Brian and Annie's family is having lunch at Marie's Restaurant. With a partner, write affirmative and negative sentences about the picture. Use the adjectives below. You can use an adjective more than one time.

hungry	young	cute	friendly
noisy	cheap	quiet	beautiful
happy	tired	sad	big

	Noun + *BE (not)*+ Adjective	Subject Pronoun + *BE (not)*+ Adjective + Noun
1.	The people are happy.	They are happy people.
2.	The baby isn't tired.	She isn't a tired baby.
3.	The boy	
4.	The girl	
5.	The waitress	
6.	Brian	
7.	The restaurant	
8.	The children	
9.		
10.		

LESSON

8 *BE* with Frequency Adverbs

Always, Usually, Often, Sometimes, Never

Use *always, usually, often, sometimes,* and *never* to talk about how often something happens. Put these words AFTER *am, is,* or *are*.

I am **always** late for work.
You are **usually** late for work.
Rose is **often** late for work.
Steve is **sometimes** * late for work.
Susan and Bob are **never** late for work.

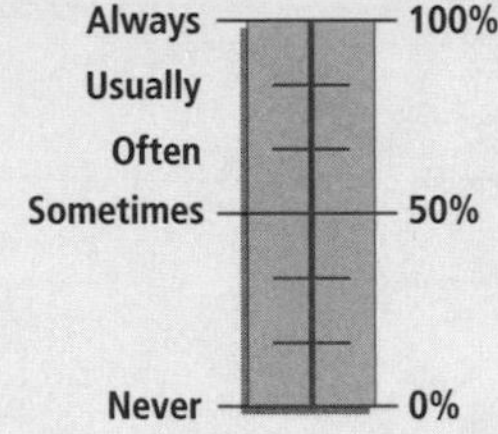

*You can put *sometimes* in three different places in a sentence.

Steve is **sometimes** late. **Sometimes** Steve is late. Steve is late **sometimes**.

A Write sentences on the lines. Use the words in parentheses. Listen to check your answers.

Susan is **early** for work.

Bob is **on time** for work.

Steve is **late** for work.

1. Susan is early for work. (always) Susan is always early for work.
2. Steve is late for work. (sometimes) ____________
3. Susan and Steve are absent from school. (sometimes) ____________
4. Mr. and Mrs. Clay are busy. (often) ____________
5. Mrs. Clay is late. (never) ____________
6. The family is at home. (often) ____________
7. The children are busy with school and work. (usually) ____________
8. Steve is at school on Mondays. (always) ____________
9. They are late for school. (usually) ____________
10. Susan is home on Saturdays. (never) ____________
11. Steve is on time for dinner. (always) ____________

B Read the paragraphs and answer the questions. Circle *T* for *True* or *F* for *False*.

1. Hi. I'm Susan. I'm usually late for school. I'm always tired in the morning. But I'm never late for work, and I'm usually on time for dinner.

Susan says . . .

a. She is usually late for school. (T) F

b. She is always late for work. T F

c. She is usually tired in the morning. T F

2. My name is Steve. I'm usually late for school. Sometimes I'm late for work. But I'm never late for dinner.

Steve says . . .

a. He is always late for school. T F

b. He is sometimes late for work. T F

c. He is always on time for dinner. T F

3. Hi. I'm Bob. Susan and Steve are my children. They're students. They're never late for school or work. Sometimes they're early! They're perfect children!

Bob says . . .

a. Susan and Steve are never late for school. T F

b. Susan and Steve are sometimes late for work. T F

c. Susan and Steve are always early. T F

C This is a list of students in Susan's class. The teacher writes ✔ when a student is on time, *A* when a student is absent, and *L* when a student is late. Work with a partner. On a separate piece of paper, write ten sentences about the students in the class. Use *always, usually, often, sometimes,* and *never.*

HISTORY 101—December

	12/2	12/4	12/6	12/9	12/11	12/13	12/16	12/18	12/20
Gina	✔	✔	✔	✔	✔	✔	✔	✔	✔
Carol	✔	A	A	✔	✔	✔	✔	✔	✔
Amy	L	A	A	✔	A	L	L	✔	A
Frank	L	✔	L	✔	✔	✔	L	L	L
Susan	L	L	✔	L	✔	L	✔	L	L
Pat	A	A	L	✔	✔	L	✔	✔	A
Larry	✔	✔	L	L	✔	✔	✔	L	✔

EXAMPLE: Gina is always on time. *OR* Gina is never late.

Lessons 5–8

Review

BE—Negative and Affirmative Statements
Adverbs of Frequency

A Dictation Listen to the conversation. Write what you hear. Then practice the conversation with a partner.
Key words: *student, busy.*

A: Are you ....

B: ....

A: ....

B: ....

B Find the mistakes. Rewrite the sentences.

1. Ellen is a person busy. — Ellen is a busy person.
2. Ellen she's a student. ....
3. Ellen is always a student good. ....
4. She also a waitress. ....
5. The restaurant great. ....
6. It is a expensive restaurant. ....
7. It no is cheap. ....
8. The waiters and waitresses busy. ....
9. The restaurant usually crowded. ....
10. The food it is good. ....
11. People is happy in the restaurant. ....
12. People no quiet in the restaurant. ....
13. She often is tired in the morning. ....
14. She never early for work. ....
15. Susan no is early for work. ....
16. Her apartment beautiful. ....
17. Her friends is often in her apartment. ....
18. Are nice people. ....
19. Sometimes they noisy. ....
20. Ellen she's a happy person. ....

C Read about Danny. Underline the verb *BE* (*is* or *isn't*). Then write the story again. Write about Danny and his twin sister, Melissa. Use *they*.

Danny is six years old. He's a happy child. He's a student in a big school. He is a good student. He isn't noisy. He isn't bad. He's never late for school. He is always on time. Sometimes he is early.

Danny and Melissa are six years old. They ....

....

....

....

....

Reminder

Don't use "a" with a plural noun.

D Get up and walk around your classroom. Ask different students these questions. When they answer, write their first names under "Yes, I am," "No, I'm not," "Yes, it is," or "No, it isn't."

You can ask: "What's your first name?" and "How do you spell it?"

Part 1

Question	Yes, I am.	No, I'm not.
EXAMPLE: Are you a student?	Mariko	....
1. Are you a teacher?	....	....
2. Are you happy today?	....	....
3. Are you tired today?	....	....
4. Are you a doctor?	....	....
5. Are you hungry?	....	....

Write five sentences about your classmates on a separate piece of paper.

EXAMPLE: Mariko is a student.

Part 2

Question	Yes, it is.	No, it isn't.
1. Is English fun?	....	....
2. Is our class difficult?	....	....
3. Is English easy?	....	....
4. Is our book big?	....	....
5. Is our classroom cold?	....	....

LESSONS 5–8

Have Fun

A Word Search Look for these words in the puzzle: *always, usually, often, sometimes,* and *never.* The words can be vertical (|), horizontal (—), or diagonal (/). The words can also be spelled backwards.

C	K	L	P	M	N	L	H	S
H	U	Y	D	E	M	A	O	E
F	R	I	V	Q	E	L	F	M
A	S	E	L	A	P	W	T	I
P	R	N	X	C	V	A	E	T
U	S	U	A	L	L	Y	N	E
J	T	I	B	Z	R	S	O	M
Y	B	D	N	N	E	T	F	O
N	I	A	C	R	T	Y	E	S

Write sentences with *am, is,* or *are.*

EXAMPLE: The students are always busy.

1. (always) I am always ______.
2. (usually) My teacher ______.
3. (often) We ______.
4. (sometimes) My family ______.
5. (never) My friends ______.

B Guessing Game Write three sentences about yourself. Use the verb *BE*. Write two *true* sentences and one *false* sentence. Read your sentences to a small group or to your class. Your classmates will guess the sentence that is false.

EXAMPLE: I am a teacher. I am not busy on weekends. I am single.

Your classmates can say: You aren't a teacher. You're a student!

1. ______
2. ______
3. ______

C Chant

She's always late.

She's *always* late.

No, she isn't.
She's *never* late.

Yes, she is.

Sometimes she's tired, but she's *always* on time.

No, she isn't.
She's *always* late.

He's *not* friendly.

Yes, he is.
He's very friendly.

No, he isn't.
He's not very nice.

Yes, he is.
He's shy,
But he's very nice.

He's a terrible cook.

No, he's not.
He's a wonderful cook.

No, he isn't.
His food is awful.

No, it's not.
It's wonderful.

He's a terrible cook.

LESSON

9 There is/There are

Prepositions of Location

Singular	Plural
There is a table in the kitchen.	There are chairs in the kitchen.
There's a table in the kitchen.* There's one table in the kitchen. * *There is* = *There's*	There are six chairs in the kitchen. *There are* = No contraction

Prepositions of Location

in	on	in front of	next to	in the corner of	near	around

A Nancy is talking to her father. Underline *there's* and *there are*. Then listen to the conversation. Practice the conversation with a partner.

Dad: Hello.

Nancy: Hi, Dad! It's Nancy. How are you?

Dad: Fine. What's new?

Nancy: We rented a house!

Dad: That's great. Is it new?

Nancy: No, it's old. But there's a nice living room and a big kitchen. And there are two small bedrooms.

Dad: That's perfect.

Nancy: There's a dining room, too. And there's a yard.

Dad: Well, congratulations. Here—your mom wants to talk to you.

Nancy: OK. Bye, Dad. . . . Hi Mom . . .

B Write about Nancy's house. Look at the picture in Exercise A. Complete the sentences with *There is* or *There are* and prepositions.

1. There is a living room.
2. There is a sofa in the living room.
3. .... a coffee table .... the sofa.
4. .... end tables .... the sofa.
5. .... pictures .... the wall.
6. .... a big kitchen.
7. .... a table .... the kitchen.
8. .... six chairs .... the table.
9. .... a refrigerator .... of the kitchen.
10. .... two pots and a pan .... the counter.
11. .... one bed .... the bedroom.
12. .... pillows .... the bed.
13. .... night tables .... the bed.
14. .... a dresser .... the door.
15. .... a TV .... the dresser.
16. .... a barbeque .... the yard.
17. .... a table .... the yard.
18. .... chairs .... the table.
19. .... flowers .... the yard.
20. .... a dog .... the yard.

C Chant

There's a table in the kitchen.

There's a table in the kitchen, yes, there is.
There's a table in the kitchen, yes, there is.
There's a table in the kitchen, yes, there is.
There's an old kitchen table in the kitchen.

There are chairs in the kitchen, yes, there are.
There are chairs in the kitchen, yes, there are.
There are chairs in the kitchen, yes, there are.
There are four kitchen chairs in the kitchen.

There are cups on the table, yes, there are.
There are cups on the table, yes, there are.
There are two coffee cups on the table,
on the kitchen table in the kitchen. Yes!

LESSON 10

BE—Yes-No Questions and Short Answers

Adjectives, Nouns, Prepositional Phrases, and Or

Statement:	You are married.		
Yes-No Question:	Are you married?		
Short Answers:	Yes, I am. No, I'm not.	(Incorrect: ~~Yes, I'm.~~)	

Yes-No Questions	Short Answers			
	Affirmative (No Contraction)	**Negative** (Contraction OK)		
Am I late?	Yes, you are.	No, you aren't.	OR	No, you're not.
Are you married?	Yes, I am.	No, I'm not.		
Is he married?	Yes, he is.	No, he isn't	OR	No, he's not.
Is she a doctor?	Yes, she is.	No, she isn't.	OR	No, she's not.
Is it good?	Yes, it is.	No, it isn't.	OR	No, it's not.
Are we late?	Yes, you are.	No, you aren't.	OR	No, you're not.
Are they at work?	Yes, they are.	No, they aren't.	OR	No, they're not.

Questions with *or*

Question: Are you married *or* single? **Answers:** I'm married.
I'm single.

A Listen. Four people are asking a famous person questions. Circle the answers you hear.

1.	Are you a man?	(Yes, I am.)	No, I'm not.
2.	Are you married?	Yes, I am.	No, I'm not.
3.	Are you an actor?	Yes, I am.	No, I'm not.
4.	Are you a musician?	Yes, I am.	No, I'm not.
5.	Are you famous?	Yes, I am.	No, I'm not.
6.	Are you old?	Yes, I am.	No, I'm not.
7.	Are you young?	Yes, I am.	No, I'm not.
8.	Are you middle-aged?	Yes, I am.	No, I'm not.
9.	Are you a politician?	Yes, I am.	No, I'm not.
10.	Is your wife Hillary?	Yes, she is.	No, she isn't.
11.	Are you Bill Clinton?	Yes, I am.	No, I'm not.

B Write Yes-No questions and answers for each picture.

1.
Question: Are they .... in a park?
Answer: Yes, they are. ....

2.
Question: .... happy?
Answer: ....

3.
Question: .... sunny?
Answer: ....

4.
Question: .... cloudy?
Answer: ....

5.
Question: .... at work?
Answer: ....

6.
Question: .... at home?
Answer: ....

Reminder

at work, at home

C Look at the pictures in Exercise B. Answer these questions.

1. Are the boys in a park or at home? They're in a park. ....
2. Are the boys happy or unhappy? ....
3. Is it sunny or cloudy? ....
4. Is the doctor at work or at home? ....
5. Is the doctor a man or a woman? ....

LESSON 11

Is there and *Are there*

Yes-No Questions with Short Answers

	Singular	Plural
Statement:	There is a school in this neighborhood.	There are schools in this neighborhood.
Yes-No Question:	Is there a school in this neighborhood?	Are there schools in this neighborhood?
Short Answers:	Yes, there is. No, there isn't.	Yes, there are. No, there aren't.

Words that show location: near, nearby, next to, two blocks away, around the corner

A Lisa and Chan are in their new apartment with their landlord. Underline questions with *Is there* and *Are there.* Circle the answers. Then listen to the conversation and practice in a group of three.

Chan: The apartment is beautiful. Are there schools near here?

Landlord: Yes, there are. There's an elementary school two blocks away. And the middle school and high school are nearby.

Lisa: Are there many kids in this building?

Landlord: Yes, there are a lot of kids.

Chan: That's good. And is there a supermarket nearby?

Landlord: Yes, there is. It's around the corner.

Lisa: Around the corner? That's great! Is there a mall?

Landlord: No, there isn't. But there are shops nearby. And there are two movie theaters next to the supermarket.

B Answer these questions about Lisa and Chan's new neighborhood. Look at Exercise A for information.

EXAMPLE: Is there an elementary school in the neighborhood? Yes, there is.

1. Is there a parking lot near the apartment building? ....
2. Is there a music store next to the apartment building? ....
3. Are there schools in the neighborhood? ....
4. Are there a lot of kids in the neighborhood? ....
5. Is there a mall near the apartment? ....
6. Are there movie theaters in the neighborhood? ....

C Write questions and answers about Lisa and Chan's new neighborhood. Look at Exercise A for information.

1. Is there a playground nearby? Yes, there is.
2. .... people in the parking lot? ....
3. .... shops in the neighborhood? ....
4. .... a movie theater around the corner from the shoe store? ....
5. .... a school next to the supermarket? ....
6. .... cars in the parking lot? ....

D Complete the questions. Then ask two classmates about where they live. Write their answers.

	Questions	Student 1	Student 2
EXAMPLE:	Is there a yard?	No, there isn't.	Yes, there is.
1.	...... there a yard?	....	....
2.	...... there a playground?	....	....
3.	...... there a movie theater in your neighborhood?	....	....
4.	...... there a supermarket in your neighborhood?	....	....
5.	...... there schools in your neighborhood?	....	....
6.	...... there shops nearby?	....	....

Lessons 9–11

Review

There is/There are Yes-No Questions with *BE*

A Dictation Listen to the paragraph about a house. Write what you hear. Key words: *living room, kitchen, yard.*

My house ....

....

....

....

B Write about your house or apartment. Use the paragraph in Exercise A as a model.

My ....

....

....

....

C Use the correct form of *BE* to complete each question. Then write short answers.

Reminder

See Appendix C for question forms with BE.

	Question	Answer
1.	Are you a student?	Yes, I am.
2.	.... you married?	....
3.	.... you at home?	....
4.	.... it sunny today?	....
5.	.... the teacher in the classroom?	....
6.	.... the door open?	....
7.	.... the windows open?	....
8.	.... the windows closed?	....
9.	.... there a lot of students in the class?	....
10.	.... the students friendly?	....
11.	.... this exercise easy?	....
12.	.... this exercise difficult?	....

D Write questions about your classroom. Then write *true* short answers. Write your own question and answer for number 6.

EXAMPLE: Is there a teacher in the classroom?
Yes, there is.

1. a clock ....
....

2. a computer ....
....

3. students ....
....

4. desks ....
....

5. windows ....
....

6. ....
....

E Put the words in the correct order. Write a statement when you see a period (.) and a question when you see a question mark (?).

1. easy/English/is ......English is easy...... .
2. easy/English/Is ....?
3. The students/friendly/are ....
4. the students/friendly/Are ....?
5. late for class/am/I/never ....
6. usually/home/We/are/at 6:00 p.m. ....
7. never/Susan/is/absent ....
8. always/on time/They/are ....

Have Fun

A Communication Gap Work with a partner. One student will be Student A and the other will be Student B.

PART 1: Student A and Student B, complete these questions with *Is there* or *Are there*. Do not write the answers now.

	Questions		Answers
1.	Is there	a TV in the living room?	....
2.	....	a couch?	....
3.	....	a lamp?	....
4.	....	pictures?	....
5.	....	a table?	....
6.	....	chairs?	....
7.	....	a computer?	....
8.	....	people?	....
9.	....	a dog?	....
10.	....	a bird?	....

PART 2

Student A: Ask Student B the questions in Part 1.
Write the answers on the lines.

Student B: Look at the picture of a living room on page 200.
Answer Student A's questions with:
Yes, there is. / *No, there isn't.* / *Yes, there are.* / *No, there aren't.*

PART 3

Student B: Ask Student A the questions in Part 1.
Write the answers on the lines.

Student A: Look at the picture of a living room on page 199.
Answer Student B's questions with:
Yes, there is. / *No, there isn't.* / *Yes, there are.* / *No, there aren't.*

B Who are you? One student and the teacher will choose the name of a famous person. The class will ask no more than 20 Yes-No questions to guess the name of the person.

Possible Questions:
1. Are you dead?
2. Are you alive?
3. Are you a woman?
4. Are you a man?

Possible Answers: Yes, I am. No, I'm not. I don't know.

C Chant

I love my town.

I love my town.
There's a lot to do.
There's a movie theater,
and a big mall, too.

Are there good restaurants?

Yes, there are,
and the great thing is, they're not very far.

There's a coffee shop. It's open at eight.
There's a grocery store. It's open late.
There's a newspaper stand. It's open at seven.
And a music store. It's open till eleven.

Are there bookstores and parks?

Yes, there are.
And the great thing is, they're not very far.

LESSON 12

Demonstrative Pronouns—*This* and *That*

Use *this* and *that* with singular nouns.

Near	**Far**
Use *this* for a person, place, or thing near (close to) you.	Use *that* for a person, place, or thing far from (not close to) you.
This is my book. (No contraction)	**That is your book.** (Contraction = *That's*)

A Listen to the conversation. Fill in the blanks with *this is* or *that's*. Then practice the conversation with a partner.

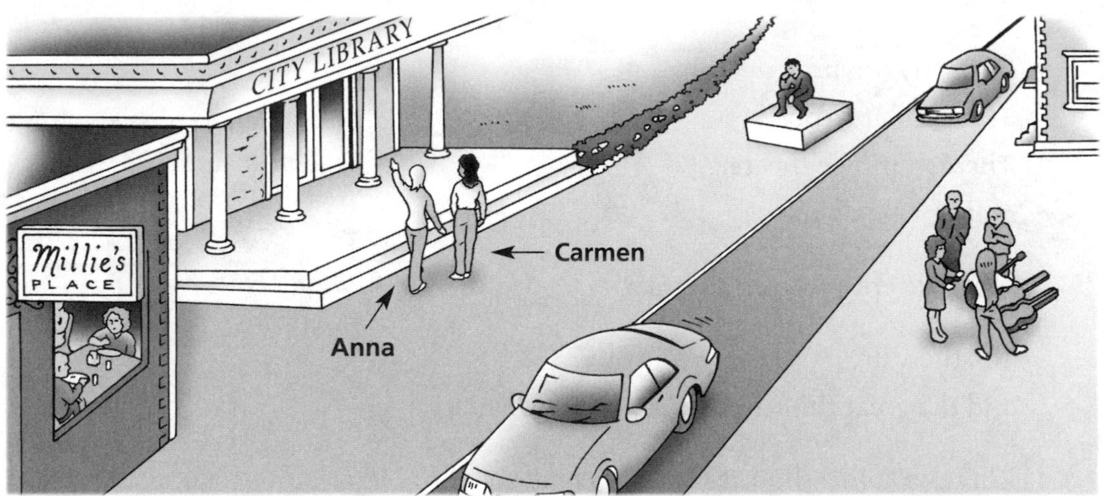

Carmen: This is a great city, Anna.

Anna: Thanks, Carmen. Oh, look—__________ the library.

Carmen: It's beautiful. What's the big building over there?

Anna: __________ City Hall. And __________ a famous park. There are a lot of concerts there in the summer.

Carmen: What's that down the street? Is that a statue?

Anna: No. __________ a person! He's a street entertainer.

Carmen: Oh, there's another entertainer across the street! She's good.

Anna: You know, it's noon. I'm hungry. Are you hungry?

Carmen: Yes, a little.

Anna: Well, __________ a good restaurant. Millie's food is delicious. Let's have lunch here.

B Read the questions about the conversation in Exercise A. Circle the answers.

1.	Is the library *close to* or *far from* the women?	close to	far from
2.	Is City Hall *close to* or *far from* the women?	close to	far from
3.	Is the park *close to* or *far from* the women?	close to	far from
4.	Are the street entertainers *close to* or *far from* the women?	close to	far from

C What is Anna saying? Complete the sentences with *This is* or *That's*.

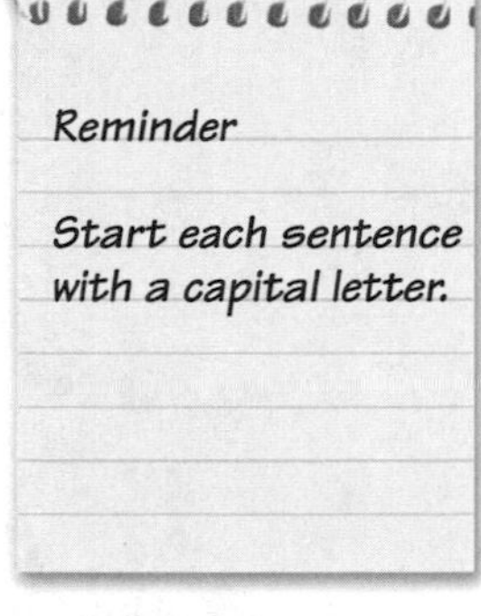

1. Anna: This is a nice museum. **2.** Anna: .... a famous clock.

3. Anna: .... a famous bridge. **4.** Anna: .... a good restaurant.

D Take turns with a partner. Put five things on your desk. (Use things in your pocket, in your purse, or in your backpack.) Follow the examples below.

First: Tell your partner what is on <u>your</u> desk.

EXAMPLE: This is my book.

Second: Tell your partner what is on <u>his</u> or <u>her</u> desk.

EXAMPLE: That's your book.

LESSON

13 Demonstrative Pronouns—*These* and *Those*

Use *these* and *those* with plural nouns.

Near	Far
Use *these* for people or things near (close to) you.	Use *those* for people or things far from (not close to) you.
These are my parents.	Those are my sisters.

A Listen to five-year-old Ricky talk about his bedroom. Circle *These are* or *Those are*.

Hi. I'm Ricky. This is my room. This is my bed. That's my closet. (1. These are / Those are) my clothes. And (2. these are / those are) my shoes. (3. These are / Those are) my fish. I have three fish. (4. These are / Those are) my books. (5. These are / Those are) my toys near the closet. My mom wants me to clean my room.

B Use the information in Exercise A to complete the sentences with *These are* and *Those are*. Then check (✔) *Close to Ricky* or *Far from Ricky*.

		Close to Ricky	Far from Ricky
1.	Those are my clothes.		✔
2.	________ my shoes.		
3.	________ my fish.		
4.	________ my toys.		
5.	________ my books.		

C Complete Ricky's sentences about his family. Write *These are* or *Those are*.

1. .... my grandparents.

2. .... my parents.

3. .... my sisters.

4. .... my brothers.

D Take turns with a partner. Put five things on your desk. (Use things in your pocket, in your purse, or in your backpack.) Point at things and say, "This is . . . ," "That is . . . ," "These are . . . ," or "Those are . . ."

First: Tell your partner what is on your desk.
For example, say: *These are my books.*

Second: Tell your partner what is on his or her desk.
For example, say: *Those are your books.*

E Chant

A Messy Room

These are here.
Those are there.
My new clothes are everywhere.

Those are my sister's sneakers there.
Those are ribbons for her hair.

These are my shoes, under my chair.
Those are my T-shirts.

Where?
Over there.

These are here, those are there.
My new clothes are everywhere!

LESSON

14 Demonstrative Pronouns—*This, That, These* and *Those*

Use *this, that, these,* and *those* with singular and plural nouns.

	Near	Far
Singular	This is my car.	That's my car.
Plural	These are my cars.	Those are my cars.

A Andrew won the lottery. Listen to him talk about his new house. Circle what you hear—*this is*, *that is*, *these are*, or *those are.*

1. (This is / That's / These are / Those are) my living room. It's beautiful.
2. (This is / That's / These are / Those are) my stereo. It's very expensive.
3. (This is / That's / These are / Those are) my CDs. I have 2000!
4. And (this is / that's / these are / those are) my TV. It's very big.
5. Let's go into the kitchen. (This is / That's / These are / Those are) my favorite room.
6. (This is / That's / These are / Those are) my new chairs. They're comfortable.
7. (This is / That's / These are / Those are) my bedroom. It's very big.
8. (This is / That's / These are / Those are) my brother's bedroom. He lives with me.
9. Look outside. (This is / That's / These are / Those are) my three cars.
10. And (this is / that's / these are / those are) my garden. Do you like my house?

B Read Andrew's sentences. Complete the chart. Check (✔) two lines for every sentence.

Andrew says:	Close To	Far From	Singular	Plural
1. *These are* my watches.	✔	______	______	✔
2. *That's* my swimming pool.	______	______	______	______
3. *This is* my boat.	______	______	______	______
4. *Those are* my computers.	______	______	______	______
5. *That's* my big TV.	______	______	______	______
6. *These are* my DVDs.	______	______	______	______
7. *This is* my garden.	______	______	______	______
8. *Those are* my motorcycles.	______	______	______	______

C What's in the bag? Take turns with a partner. Put five things into a bag. Tell your partner to close his or her eyes, take things out of the bag, and say what they are.

One student: This is a(n) ______________ . OR

These are ______________ .

The other student: Yes, you're right. OR

No, you're wrong. Try again.

D What's on the teacher's desk? Put one or two things on your teacher's desk. Your teacher will point to different things on the desk. When your teacher calls on you, say: "That's a(n) ______________ ." OR "Those are ______________ ."

LESSON 15

This, That, These, and *Those*

Yes-No Questions with Short Answers
Possessive Adjectives (my, your, his, her)

Use *this, that, these,* or *those* to ask a question about a singular or plural noun.

Statement:	That	is	your book.
Yes-No Question:	Is	that	your book?

Questions	Short Answers (Use *it* or *they* in your answers.)	
	Affirmative	Negative
Is **this** your book? Is **that** your book?	Yes, **it** is.	No, **it** isn't. OR No, **it**'s not.
Are **these** your books? Are **those** your books?	Yes, **they** are.	No, **they** aren't. OR No, **they**'re not.

A Bill, Will, and Phil are roommates. They are cleaning their room. Underline the questions with *this, that, these,* and *those*. Listen to the conversation. Then practice the conversation with two partners.

Bill: Will, is this your CD?

Will: Yes, it is! It's great! Let's listen to it now.

Bill: OK. Hey, Phil! Is that your clock under the bed?

Phil: No, it isn't. My clock is on the table.

Will: Oh, that's my clock under the bed.

Bill: Why is it under the bed?

Will: I don't know.

Phil: Hey, Bill—are these your keys?

Bill: Yes, they are! Thanks! Are those your socks, Phil?

Phil: No, they're not. They're very dirty. Hey, Will! That's my toothbrush!

Will: Oh, sorry. But it's dirty. This room is a mess!

B Change these statements into Yes-No questions.

1. This is your CD. Is this your CD?
2. These are my socks. ....
3. That's his shirt. ....
4. Those are my shoes. ....
5. This is my watch. ....
6. That's her TV. ....
7. These are your keys. ....
8. Those are her keys. ....

C Bill, Will, and Phil did their laundry together. Read their conversation. Cross out the mistakes in the questions. Make corrections.

Bill: ~~This is~~ Is this your shirt, Phil?

Phil: Yes, it is. These are your socks?

Bill: No, they aren't.

Phil: Will, these are your socks?

Will: Yes, they are. And those are my jeans.

Phil: No, they're *my* jeans!

Will: Oh, you're right. That is my shirt?

Bill: Yes, it is. These are your shorts?

Phil: No, they aren't. Those are *my* shorts.

D Work in a group of four. Three students will each put two things into a bag. The fourth student will take things out of the bag and ask the other students questions. Put new things in the bag and take turns being the fourth student.

EXAMPLES: A: Is this your pen, Mario?

B: Yes, it is.

A: Are these your keys, Kim?

B: No, they aren't.

LESSON

16 *This*, *That*, *These*, and *Those*

Questions with What

Use *what* to ask a question about a singular or plural noun.

Statement:		That	is	a telephone.
Yes-No Question:		Is	that	a telephone?
What Question:	What	is	that?	

Questions	**Answers** (Use it or they in your answers.)
What is (What's) this?	It's a telephone.
What is (What's) that?	It's a telephone.
What are these?	They're telephones.
What are those?	They're telephones.

A Mr. Van Winkle slept for 200 years. Lydia is showing him things we use today. Listen to the conversation. Fill in the blanks with *this*, *that*, *these*, or *those*. Practice the conversation with a partner.

Mr. Van Winkle: What's ___this___?

Lydia: It's an MP3 player.

Mr. Van Winkle: What's an MP3 player?

Lydia: It's a machine. It plays music.

Mr. Van Winkle: OK. And what's __________?

Lydia: It's a TV.

Mr. Van Winkle: What are __________?

Lydia: Over there? Oh, they're computers.

Mr. Van Winkle: And what are __________?

Lydia: They're headphones. You use them with an MP3 player. Try them.

Mr. Van Winkle: Hmmm. Very nice!

Lydia: I'll buy an MP3 player for you. It's a present!

B Look at the pictures. Write questions and answers.

1.

Q: What's this?

A: It's a telephone.

2.

Q: ......

A: ......

3.

Q: ......

A: ...... stereos.

4.

Q: ......

A: ......

5.

Q: ......

A: ...... TVs.

6.

Q: ......

A: ......

7.

Q: ......

A: ......

8.

Q: ......

A: ......

C Work with a partner. Take turns being Mr. Van Winkle and Lydia. Ask and answer six questions about things in your classroom. Use *What's this/that?* and *What are these/those?* When you finish, write your conversations.

EXAMPLE: Mr. Van Winkle: What's this?

Lydia: It's a notebook.

Lessons 12–16

Review

Demonstrative Pronouns

A Dictation Listen to the conversation. Write what you hear. Then practice the conversation with a partner. Key words: *pen, keys.*

A: Is this ....

B: ....

A: ....

B: ....

B Lisa is showing Brian photos of her family. Underline the correct words.

Lisa: (This is / <u>These are</u>) my parents.

Brian: They look very happy.

Lisa: And (this is / these are) my older brother.

Brian: He's handsome. (Is this / Are these) your children?

Lisa: No, (it's / they're) not. They're (your / my) grandchildren.

Brian: Wow. You look too young to be a grandmother! What is (that / those)?

Lisa: Oh, (that's / those are) a famous art museum.

Brian: (Is this / Are these) your friends?

Lisa: Yes, (it is / they are).

Brian: (This is / These are) wonderful photos.

Lisa: Thank you.

C Complete the chart with singular or plural statements or questions. Use periods (.) for statements and question marks (?) for questions.

	Singular	Plural
1.	This is my DVD.	These are my DVDs.
2.	....	Those are my classmates.
3.	....	Are these your books?
4.	Is that your car?	....
5.	What's this?	....
6.	....	What are those?

D Write a Yes-No question with *this*, *that*, *these*, or *those* for each drawing. Answer each question with "Yes . . ."

1.

Are those your roommates?

Yes, they are.

2.

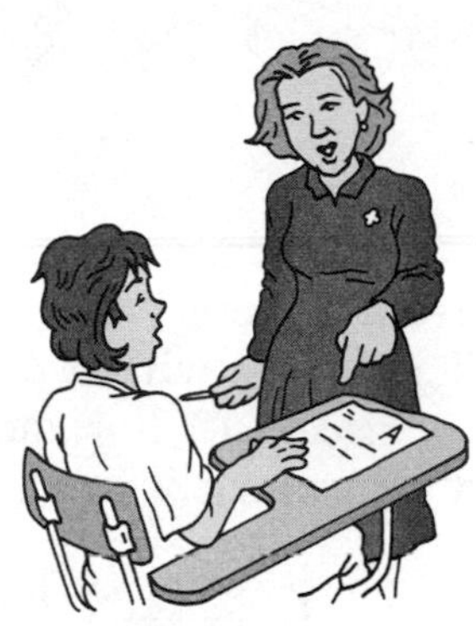

.... your test?

....

3.

....

....

4.

....

....

5.

....

....

6.

.... the Eiffel Tower?

....

LESSONS 12–16

Have Fun

A Word Search Write "This is my . . ." or "These are my . . ." before each word. Then work with a partner and find the nouns in the puzzle. The words can be vertical (|), horizontal (—), or diagonal (/). The words can also be spelled backwards.

This is my	apartment.		house.
	bed.		keys.
	bedroom.		neighbors.
	brothers.		parents.
	clothes.		school.
	desk.		shoes.
	garden.		socks.

G	B	A	D	Y	D	C	T	L	S
A	R	M	G	E	L	F	N	S	T
R	O	L	S	O	B	E	E	J	N
D	T	K	T	J	E	S	M	V	E
E	H	H	F	A	T	U	T	P	R
N	E	I	G	H	B	O	R	S	A
S	R	S	Y	E	K	H	A	O	P
M	S	C	H	O	O	L	P	C	N
S	E	O	H	S	R	A	A	K	C
M	O	O	R	D	E	B	I	S	L

B Bring in three big pictures of things from magazines or newspapers. Take turns showing them to your class. Your classmates will ask you "What's that?" and "What are those?" Answer your classmates' questions.

EXAMPLE: Student B: What's that?

Student A: It's a CD player.

Student C: (points to another picture) What are those?

Student A: They're tennis shoes.

C Chant

Is this your sweater?

Is this your sweater?
No, that's his.
Is this your book bag?
Yes, it is.

Are these your keys?
Yes, they are.
Those are my keys.
And that's my car.

What's this?
It's my mailbox key.
What's that?
It's a letter for me.

Is that your credit card?
Yes, it is.
Are those your packages?
No, they're his.

Is that a photo of Susan?
No, that's Liz.
Is this a picture of you?
Yes, it is.

LESSON 17

Questions with *What's*

*Possessive Adjectives (*my/your/his/her*)*

Long and Short Answers

Use *What* to ask for information.

What*-Questions** ***(What's = What is)	**Long Answers**	**Short Answers**
What's your name? What's his name? What's her name?	My name is Helen. His name is Tom. Her name is Olivia.	(It's) Helen. (It's) Tom. (It's) Olivia.

Expressions	
I think . . .	I'm not sure.

A Listen to the conversation between Mary and her brother Tony. Fill in the blanks with *his* or *her*. Then practice the conversation with a partner.

Mary: Look behind you! There are the stars of *San Francisco*!

Tony: What's that?

Mary: You know—it's a TV show!

Tony: Hmm, she's beautiful. What's .... name?

Mary: It's Olivia, I think. I'm not sure.

Tony: What's .... last name?

Mary: Rivera.

Tony: How about the guy? What's .... name?

Mary: It's Tom. And I think .... last name is Newman.

Tony: Are they married?

Mary: No, they're not.

B Look at Olivia Rivera's driver's license. Complete the questions and write long answers.

California
Olivia Rosa Rivera
Address: 2630 Beach Avenue
Beverly Hills, CA 90210
Hair: Brown
Eyes: Brown
Date of Birth: 7-5-1972
License #: N9234857
Expires: 7-5-2012

1. What's .... her last name?
   Her last name is Rivera.
2. .... her middle name?
   ....
3. .... her address?
   ....
4. .... her date of birth?
   ....
5. .... her license number?
   ....

C Write questions to ask a classmate. Then interview a classmate.

1. What's your .... first name? ....
2. .... last name? ....
3. .... address? ....
4. .... phone number? ....

Now write sentences about your classmate on a separate piece of paper. Read your sentences to a different classmate.

EXAMPLE: Her first name is Helen.

D Chant

What's his name?

What's his name?
His name is Harry.
What's her name?
Her name is Mary.

What's his name?
I think it's Joe.
What's his last name?
I don't know.

What's your mother's first name?
Jill.
What's your father's first name?
Bill.

LESSON 18

Questions with *Where*

Prepositions of Location
Answers with Subject Pronouns

Use *Where* to ask about location.

	***Where*-Questions**	**Answers**
Things:	Where is (Where's) my wallet?	It's on the table.
	Where are my keys?	They're in the kitchen.
People:	Where am I?	You're at school.
	Where are you?	I'm at home.
		We're at home.
	Where is he?	He's in his bedroom.
	Where is she?	She's at work.
	Where are we?	We're at Andy's house.
	Where are they?	They're in Mexico.
	Where's Molly?*	She's in the backyard.
	Where are Katie and Andy?	They're in the kitchen.

*You can use the contraction *where's* with a name or a noun.

Language Notes

Probably: Say *probably* when you are not 100% sure.
A: Where's your sister?
B: I'm not sure. She's *probably* at work. She usually works on Mondays.

A Fill in the blanks with *is* or *are*. Then listen and practice with a partner.

1. Molly: Where ..is.. my pen?
   Andy: It's on the table, Mom.
2. Molly: Where .... my glasses?
   Andy: They're on top of your head!
3. Molly: Where .... my keys?
   Andy: They're in your pocket!
4. Molly: And where .... my car?
   Andy: It's in the garage!
5. Molly: Where .... Katie?
   Andy: She's in her bedroom.
6. Molly: Where .... your father?
   Andy: He's at work.

B Look at the pictures of Molly, Charlie, Katie, and Andy. Complete their questions and write answers. Use the list of places for your answers.

PLACES
on the counter
in the kitchen
on the floor
at school
at work
in the living room

1\.

Andy: *Where are* my books?
You: *They're on the floor.*

2\.

Charlie: .... the potatoes?
You: ....

3\.

Molly: .... Charlie?
You: ....

4\.

Charlie: .... Molly?
You: ....

5\.

Molly: .... Katie and Andy?
You: ....

6\.

Andy: .... Tuck?
You: ....

C On a separate piece of paper, write *Where* questions and answers about four friends or people in your family. Use *probably* in your answers. When you finish, practice your questions and answers with a partner.

EXAMPLE: Q: *Where's Rosa?*
A: *She's probably at work.*

LESSON 19

Questions with *Where* and *What*

Countries, Nationalities, and Languages

Possessive Adjectives (my/your/his/her/their)

Questions				Long Answers	Short Answers
Where	are	you	from?	I'm from New York.	New York.
	is	he		He's from Peru.	Peru.
	are	they		They're from China.	China.
What's	your		nationality?	I'm American.	American.
	his			He's Peruvian.	Peruvian.
	their			They're Chinese.	Chinese.
What's	your		first language?	My first language is English.	English.
	her			Her first language is Korean.	Korean.

A Read about Melissa's neighborhood. Underline the countries, nationalities, and languages. Listen to the paragraphs, and then take turns reading them with a partner.

Hi! My name is Melissa. I live in a very international neighborhood. It's great. I'm <u>American</u>—I'm from the U.S. and I speak English.

My next-door neighbors, Rika and Hiroshi, are from Japan. They speak Japanese. They often make delicious Japanese food for me. My other next-door neighbors, Ana and Daniel, are from Mexico. They speak Spanish. I like my neighbors a lot.

There are many international restaurants in our neighborhood. There are two Mexican restaurants, three Chinese restaurants, an Indian restaurant, and an Iranian restaurant. People from Mexico work in the Mexican restaurants. People from China work in the Chinese restaurants. People from India work in the Indian restaurant. And people from Iran work in the Iranian restaurant.

I love my international neighborhood.

B Write questions about these people from Exercise A. Use *Where* or *What* and subject pronouns or possesive adjectives (*his*, *her*, *their*) in your questions. Then complete the answers.

Melissa	**1.** Where is she from? .... She's from .... **2.** .... Her first language is ....
Rika	**3.** .... nationality? She's .... **4.** .... She's from ....
Ana and Daniel	**5.** .... nationality? They are .... **6.** .... first language? Their first language is ....

C Complete the first line of the chart below with information about you. Then ask four of your classmates these questions. Complete the chart with information about your classmates.

See Appendix F for spelling of countries, nationalities, and languages.

Questions to ask: What's your name?
Where are you from?
What's your nationality?
What's your first language?

	Name	Country	Nationality	First Language
1.	(you)			
2.				
3.				
4.				
5.				

Now write sentences about you and your five classmates.

EXAMPLES:
- I'm from Vietnam. I'm Vietnamese. My first language is Vietnamese.
- Tatiane and Luciane are from Brazil. They're Brazilian. Their first language is Portuguese.

LESSON

20 Questions with *When* and *What Time*

In/On/At *and Possessive Adjectives*

Questions		Long Answers	Short Answers
When	is your birthday?	My birthday is (on) June 25. It's (on) June 25. It's on Monday. It's in June.	June 25. June 25. On Monday. In June.
What time	is your party? is it?	It's at 8:00. It's 2:30.	At 8:00. 2:30.

Language Notes

- Use *on* with a day or date. Use *in* with a month. Use *at* with a time.
  on Monday   in June   at 8:00
- When you say a date, like "June 25," pronounce it "June twenty-fifth."

Subject Pronouns	Possessive Adjectives
I	my
you	your (for singular and plural)
he	his
she	her
we	our
they	their

A Listen to the conversation. Write *When* or *What time* on the lines. Then practice the conversation with a partner.

Joan: Hi, Ellen. Hi, Ken. What time ________ is your flight to New York?
Ellen: It's at 11:00 p.m.
Joan: ________ is your meeting with Mr. Kim, Ellen?
Ellen: It's on Tuesday. ________ is *your* trip to New York?
Joan: It's in July.
Ken: Hey, ________ is our meeting today?
Joan: It's at 2:00. ________ is it?
Ken: It's 1:45.
Joan: Oh! Let's go.

B Fill in the blanks with *in, on, or at.*

1. My appointment is ......at...... 3 o'clock. I'm in a hurry.
2. Our anniversary is .... August. We want a big party.
3. Our anniversary is .... August 1.
4. Her birthday is .... Saturday.
5. His birthday party is .... 7:30.
6. Their party is .... Sunday .... 4 o'clock.

C Write questions with *When* or *What time* about the people in Exercise A, and complete the answers. Use the possessive adjectives *her* or *their*. Use the prepositions *in*, *on*, or *at*.

1. about Ellen: Q: When is her meeting with Mr. Kim?
   A: .... meeting is .... Tuesday.
2. about Joan: Q: ....
   A: .... trip is .... July.
3. about Ellen and Ken: Q: ....
   A: .... flight is .... 11:00.
4. about Ellen, Ken, and Joan: Q: ....
   A: It's .... 2:00.

D Take turns asking a partner questions and giving possible answers. Use the words in the boxes below. Be careful—use *What time is* ... only to ask about a specific time.

Questions		Possible Answers
What time is	the test?	At 3:30.
	his party?	At 8:00 p.m.
	our appointment?	At 10:00 a.m.
When is	their anniversary?	On Tuesday.
	your birthday?	On May 13.
	her wedding?	In February.

EXAMPLE: Q: When is your birthday?
A: On May 13.

LESSON

21 Questions with *How is* and *How are*

Answers with Adjectives

	Questions	Answers	
Asking about the weather:	How is the weather? How's the weather?	It's sunny. It's cloudy. It's rainy. It's foggy. It's windy.	It's hot. It's warm. It's cool. It's cold.
Asking about things and people:	How is your soup? How are your kids?	It's great/fine/OK/not very good. They're great/fine/busy.	

A Chris and his family are on vacation. Read these e-mail messages about their trip. Fill in the blanks with *How is* or *How are*. Then listen to check your answers.

From: workalot@mcg.com
To: chrism@pacmail.net
Subject: your vacation
Sent: 4/3/07 9:27 AM

Hi Chris,

.... the beach? .... the weather? It's cold and cloudy here. .... your kids? I'm sure they love the beach.

See you on Monday at work. Have a great time!
Pat

From: chrism@pacmail.net
To: workalot@mcg.com
Subject: RE: your vacation
Sent: 4/4/07 6:02 PM

Hi Pat,

The beach is great! The weather is beautiful. It's sunny and warm in the morning and in the afternoon. It's cool at night. The beach isn't crowded and the kids are very happy.

.... you? .... work? When is your next vacation?

See you soon,
Chris

B Chris and his family are at a restaurant. Complete the questions with *How is* or *How are*. Complete the answers with *It's* or *They're*.

1.

Chris: How is .... your hamburger?
Max: It's .... delicious.

2.

Chris: .... your eggs?
Kathy: .... not bad.

3.

Chris: .... your fries?
Sally: .... very good.

4.

Chris: .... your soup?
Kathy: .... spicy.

5.

Chris: .... your vegetables?
Max: .... terrible!

5.

Chris: .... your pancakes?
Max: .... cold.

7.

Chris: .... your sandwich?
Sally: .... great.

8.

Chris: .... your salad?
Kathy: .... OK.

C Answer these questions about the weather where you live now.

EXAMPLE: How is the weather today? It's rainy.

1. How's the weather today? ....
2. How's the weather at night? ....
3. How's the weather in April? ....
4. How's the weather in October? ....
5. How's the weather in February? ....
6. How's the weather in August? ....

Lessons 17–21

Review

Wh Questions with *BE*

A Dictation Listen to the conversation about a birthday. Write what you hear. Key words: *present, birthday.*

A: What's ....

B: ....

A: ....

B: ....

B Read the information about David Hernandez. Write questions with *when, where, what, what time,* and *how*.

GRAMMAR 1 STUDENT INFORMATION CARD

Name: David Hernandez **Address:** 1505 Maple St.
City: Springfield **State:** Ohio
Country: USA **Nationality:** Mexican
First Language: Spanish **Birthday:** March 16, 1975
Class: Grammar **Time:** Monday 7:00 – 10:00 p.m.
Do you like your writing class? Yes, it's very good.
Do you like your other classes? Yes, my other classes are great.

1. Q: What's his name?
A: His name is David Hernandez.

2. Q: ....
A: His address is 1505 Maple St.

3. Q: ....
A: He's from Mexico.

4. Q: ....
A: His first language is Spanish.

5. Q: ....
A: His nationality is Mexican.

6. Q: ....
A: His birthday is on March 16.

7. Q: ....
A: His class is on Monday.

8. Q: ....
A: His class is from 7:00 to 10:00.

9. Q: ....
A: His writing class is very good.

10. Q: ....
A: His classes are great!

C Write *in, on*, or *at.*

Prepositions of Time		
in in June	.... July	.... 8 a.m.
.... Thursday	.... January 1st	.... July 21st
.... midnight	.... Tuesday	.... 9 p.m.

Prepositions of Location		
.... the living room	.... the kitchen	.... school
.... the table	.... the floor	.... the bathroom
.... my pocket	.... home	.... work

D Olivia has some pictures of her family. Complete the sentences with *my, his, her,* or *their.*

1. Hi. My name is Olivia. Here are some photos of .... family.

2. This is .... brother and this is .... wife. They live in New York with .... two children.

3. This is .... sister and .... new boyfriend.

4. These are .... parents. They live in Peru, but all .... children live in the U.S.

LESSONS 17–21

Have Fun

A Crossword Puzzle

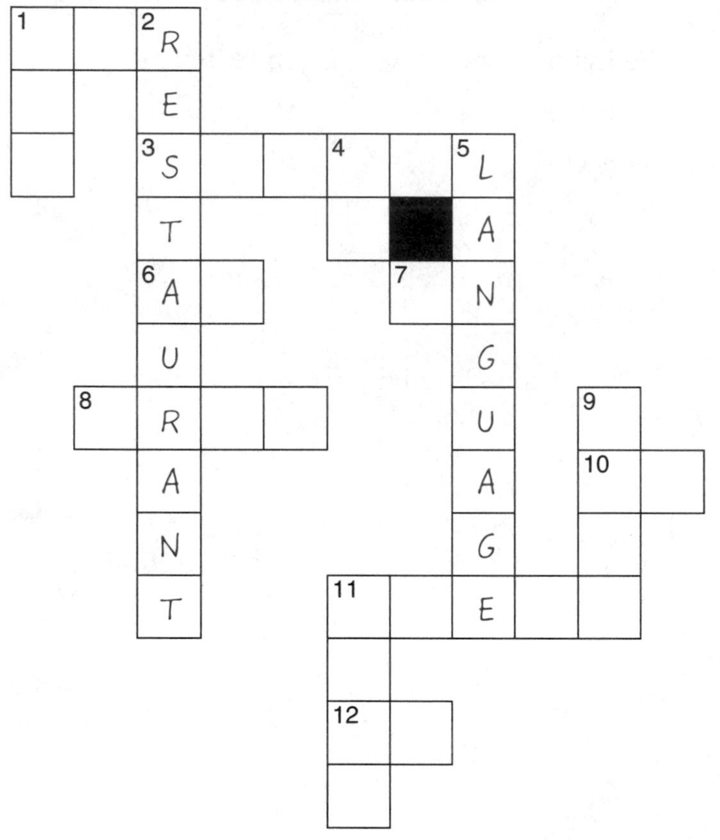

Across

1. I have a sister. .... name is Janet.
3. I study English at ....
6. The class is .... 8:00.
7. He's .... the living room.
8. Where are you .... ?
10. Where .... your teacher?
11. .... are you from?
12. Where .... I?

Down

1. I have a brother. .... name is David.
2. I eat every day at this ....
4. Your keys are .... the table.
5. What's your first .... ?
9. What .... is it?
11. .... is your address?

B Chant

What's your name? Where are you from?

What's your name?
My name is Jane.
Where are you from?
I'm from Maine.

How's the summer in Maine?
Is it sunny and hot?

Sometimes it is
And sometimes it's not.

How's the winter in Maine?
Is there lots of snow?

Yes, there is?
I want to go.
When's the best time to visit?
Is it nice in May?

Maine's always nice
For a holiday.

LESSON 22

Demonstrative Adjectives *This*, *That*, *These*, and *Those*

Singular and Plural Nouns

	Near	Far
Singular	this jacket	that jacket
Plural	these jackets	those jackets

Spelling of Regular Plural Nouns

Add *s* to most nouns	**Add *es* to nouns that end in *s, ss, ch, sh, x,* and *z***
jacket ⟶ jackets store ⟶ stores	dress ⟶ dresses watch ⟶ watches

A Underline *this, that, these*, and *those* and the nouns that follow them. Listen to the conversation. Practice the conversation in a group of three.

Sam:	This store is really crowded today.
Bina:	You're right. It *is* crowded. Look—these shoes are nice.
Sam :	They're OK. Are they expensive?
Bina :	Yes, they are. Maybe those shoes over there aren't expensive.
Sam :	The black shoes on the table? How much are they?
Bina :	I don't know. There's a salesperson . . . Excuse me. How much are these shoes?
Salesperson:	I'm not sure. I think they're around forty dollars. . . No, they're on sale. They're twenty-five dollars today!
Bina :	Great! I'll try them on.
Salesperson:	What size are you?
Bina :	Uh, I think size eight.
Salesperson:	OK. I'll be right back.

B Read the sentences. Complete the chart. Check two lines for every sentence.

	Near	Far	Singular	Plural
1. These jeans are great.	✔			✔
2. That T-shirt is cheap.				
3. These clothes are expensive.				
4. This store is crowded.				
5. Those customers aren't friendly.				
6. These glasses are nice.				

These words are always plural: clothes, jeans, pants, shorts, glasses

C Make sentences 1–3 plural. Make sentences 4–6 singular.

1. This jacket is expensive.

These jackets are expensive.

2. That watch isn't big.

3. That belt is brown.

4. These dresses are beautiful.

5. Those suits aren't your size.

6. These coats aren't warm.

Reminder

Don't add "s" to adjectives when they describe plural nouns.

D Walk around your classroom with a partner. Talk about what you see. Use *this*, *that*, *these*, and *those*. When you finish, write five sentences.

EXAMPLE: This desk is small. That book is blue.
These pencils are new. Those windows are big.

LESSON 23 Questions with *How much* and *How old*

Questions	Answers
How much is this/that lamp? How much are these/those lamps?	(It's) $12.50. (They're) $15 each.
How old is this/that lamp? How old is it? How old are these/those lamps? How old are they?	(It's) About ten years old. (They're) About ten years old.
How old is John? How old are you?	(He's) Thirty./ He's thirty years old. (I'm) Five./I'm five years old.

Language Notes

Incorrect: ~~He has thirty years./I have thirty years.~~
~~He's thirty years./I'm thirty years.~~

A Fill in the blanks with *is* or *are*. Then listen to this conversation at a flea market. Practice the conversation in a group of three.

Woman:	Hi. Can I help you?
Man:	Yes. How much ____is____ this lamp?
Woman:	It's $12.50.
Man:	It's very nice, but it's small. How much ________ those two big lamps over there?
Woman:	They're $15 each.
Man:	How old ________ they?
Woman:	Oh, about ten years old. . . . Hi honey. How old ________ you?
Little Girl:	I'm five.
Woman:	And how old ________ your little brother?
Little Girl:	He's one.
Woman:	You're a very nice big sister. . . . Sir, I can give you the two big lamps for $25.
Man:	How about $20?
Woman:	$23?
Man:	OK. Here's ten, twenty, one, two, three…

B Look at Exercise A and answer these questions in complete sentences. Say the questions and answers with a partner.

1. Q: How much is the small lamp? A: It's $12.50
2. Q: How much are the two big lamps at the beginning of the conversation? A: ....
3. Q: How much are the two big lamps at the end of the conversation? A: ....
4. Q: How old are the two lamps? A: ....
5. Q: How old is the little girl? A: ....
6. Q: How old is the baby boy? A: ....

C Look at the picture of a table at a flea market. Write questions about the things on the table.

1. Q: How much is the radio? A: It's $5.
2. Q: ....? A: It's $100.
3. Q: ....? A: The typewriter is sixty years old.
4. Q: ....? A: The telephones are about fifty years old.
5. Q: ....? A: The telephones are $25 each.
6. Q: ....? A: The dishes are $18.
7. Q: ....? A: The big vase is $14.
8. Q: ....? A: The small vase is $2.

LESSON

24 Questions with *Who*

Short Answers and Who else is . . . ?

Use *Who's* to ask about people.

	Questions	Possible Answers	
		Singular	**Plural**
With nouns:	**Who's a teacher?** **Who's a student?**	**You are.** **I am.**	**You are.** **We are.**
With adjectives:	**Who's hungry?** **Who's absent today?**	**I am.** **Amy is.**	**We are.** **Amy and May are.**
With places:	**Who's at the board?** **Who's in the classroom?** **Who's from Mexico?**	**She is.** **Johnny is.** **Mario is.**	**Lynn and I are.** **They are.** **Mario and Anna are.**

Use *Who else is* to ask about more people.

Who else is a student? **Who else is hungry?** **Who else is at the board?**

A Read the questions and answers. Listen and match the answers to the questions. You can use the answers more than one time.

a	**1.** Who's a teacher?	**a.**	Suzanne is.
......	**2.** Who's very funny?	**b.**	Angelica and Mario are.
......	**3.** Who's married?	**c.**	Benjamin is.
......	**4.** Who's from China?	**d.**	Olga is.
......	**5.** Who else is from China?	**e.**	Nooshi is.
......	**6.** Who's always busy?	**f.**	Chang is.
......	**7.** Who's from Russia?	**g.**	Cai is.
......	**8.** Who's an artist?	**h.**	Ly is.
......	**9.** Who's from Iran?		

B Write a question with *Who's* or *Who else is* under each picture. Use information from Exercise A.

1. Q: Who's a doctor?
   A: Benjamin is.

2. Q: ....
   A: Chang is.

3. Q: .... Mexico?
   A: Angelica is.

4. Q: .... Mexico?
   A: Mario is.

C Write questions with *Who's* and *Who else is* to ask about your classmates. Then walk around your classroom and ask your classmates to answer your questions. Write their answers on the right.

	Questions	Short Answers
EXAMPLE:	Who is a mother? Who else is a mother?	Christina and Mai Li are. Linda is.
1.	Who is (noun)	....
	Who else is	....
2.	(adjective)	....
	....	....
3.	(place)	....
	....	....

D Chant

Where is everybody?

Who's absent today?
Bobby and Ray.
Who else is absent?
Sally and Fay.
Who's at the blackboard?
Billy is.

Who's in the office?
Larry and Liz.
Who's from Moscow?
Olga is.
Who's from Dallas?
Sally and Liz.

Who's always here?
Billy is.
Who's always early?
Olga and Liz.

LESSON

25 Questions with *When*, *What time*, and *How long*

Answers with at, on, around, *and* from ____ to ____

Questions	Answers
When is the movie?	(It's) At 7:00. (It's) On Friday. (at 7:00)
What time is the movie?	(It's) At 7:00. (It's) From 7:00 to 9:00. I think it's around 7:00. (around 7:00)
How long is the movie?	Two hours. It's two hours long.

A Read the conversation. Underline the questions with *when*, *what time*, and *how long*. Listen to the conversation. Practice with a partner.

TIMES
7:00
7 o'clock

Jackie

Tony

Ring...

Tony: Hello.

Jackie: Hi, Tony. It's Jackie. How are you?

Tony: Oh, hi, Jackie. I'm fine. How are you?

Jackie: Not bad. Listen, there's a good movie at the Albany Theatre. Do you want to see it?

Tony: When is it?

Jackie: Saturday.

Tony: What time?

Jackie: At 7:00.

Tony: How long is the movie? I need to be home at 10:00 on Saturday.

Jackie: I don't know. It's probably about two hours—from 7:00 to 9:00.

Tony: OK. Let's go.

Jackie: Great! I'll pick you up at 6:30 on Saturday.

Tony: Great. See you on Saturday. Bye.

Jackie: See you. Bye.

B Complete the conversations with the prepositions: *at, on,* and *from . . . to*.

Sue: Jackie, when is your date with Tony?

Jackie: It's .... Saturday.

Sue: What time is the movie?

Jackie: It's .... 7:00.

Sue: How long is the movie?

Jackie: About two hours. It's .... 7:00 .... 9:00.

Tony: Jackie, when's your exercise class?

Jackie: It's .... Friday mornings. Are you interested?

Tony: Well, maybe. How long is the class?

Jackie: Only forty-five minutes. It's .... 8:00 .... 8:45.

Tony: That's early! I get up .... 9:00 every day!

Jackie: I think there's also a class .... 10:00 or 11:00.

C Write questions. Then ask three students your questions and write their answers.

Questions	**Answers**
EXAMPLE:	
When is your birthday?	In March.
When is	1. ....
	2. ....
	3. ....
What time is	1. ....
	2. ....
	3. ....
How long is	1. ....
	2. ....
	3. ....

Reminder

Use "on" with days.

Use "in" with months.

LESSON 26 There/Their/They're

There, Their and *They're* are different words. The pronunciation of these words is exactly the same.

THERE

(1) Use *there* to talk about a place.
- **They like the zoo. They are there now.**
- **It's (over) there.**

(2) Use *there is/there are* to talk about something in a place.
- **There is (There's) a monkey at the zoo.**
- **There are monkeys at the zoo.**

THEIR

Use *their* to show possession.
- **Their grandchildren are very young.**
- **Bob and Anne are in their car.**

THEY'RE

***They're* is the contraction of *They are*.**
- **They're grandparents.**
- **They're very happy.**
- **They're in the kitchen.**

A Read this story for children. Underline the words *there*, *their*, and *they're*. Count them and write the numbers in the chart. Then listen to the story.

Grandma and Grandpa are at the zoo with <u>their</u> two grandchildren, Diana and Larry. They're all very happy. There is a big section with monkeys. When they go there, Diana says, "Look over there! There are three baby monkeys! Their mother is under the tree with them." Larry says, "And their father is there too. He's in the tree. They're all together."

There (place)	There is/There are	Their	They're
3	....	....	....

B Fill in the blanks with *there, their,* or *they're.*

1. Their grandmother is 70 years old.
2. ________ are two children in ________ family.
3. ________ young.
4. ________ is a monkey in the tree.
5. ________ at the zoo.
6. ________ is a gorilla over ________ .
7. ________ is one gorilla over here, and ________ are two gorillas over ________ .
8. ________ big gorillas.
9. The children and ________ grandfather are happy today.

C Six sentences have mistakes with *there, their* and *they're*. Find the mistakes. Rewrite the sentences. If a sentence is correct, write *correct*.

1. *There* car is hot. It's in the sun. Their car is hot. It's in the sun.
2. Their thirsty. They want water. ________
3. Their parents aren't at the zoo. ________
4. They're grandparents are at the zoo. ________
5. There at the gift shop. ________
6. Monkeys are their favorite animals. ________
7. Their parents aren't their. ________
8. They're at the zoo every Sunday. ________
9. It's time for lunch. There hungry. ________
10. Their lunch is delicious. ________

AUDIO

D **Dictation** Listen to three sentences. Write what you hear. Think about *there, their* and *they're.*

1. ________
2. ________
3. ________

Lessons 22–26

Review

Demonstrative Adjectives

Wh Questions with BE

There/Their/They're

A Dictation Listen to the conversation in a shoe store. Write what you hear. Then practice the conversation with a partner. Key words: *shoes, beautiful, on sale.*

A: These shoes ....

B: ....

A: ....

B: ....

A: ....

B Look at Maria's calendar. Then answer the questions. Use *long, on, at,* and *from ___ to ___* in your answers.

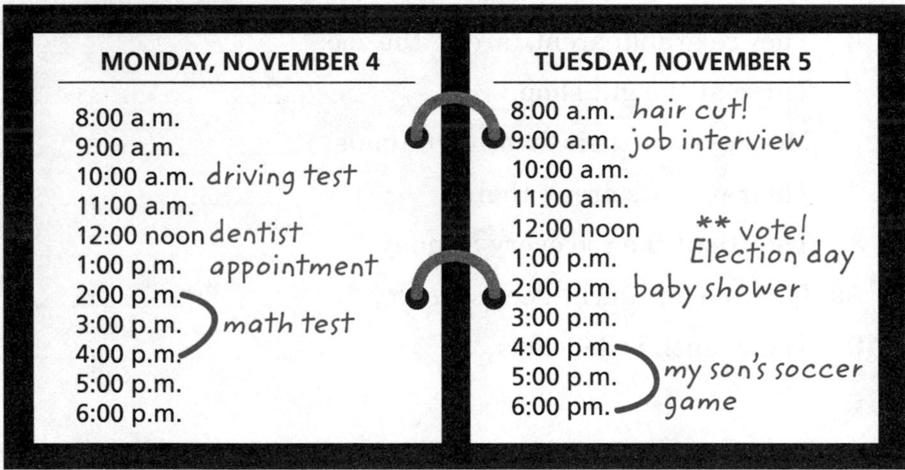

MONDAY, NOVEMBER 4
8:00 a.m.
9:00 a.m.
10:00 a.m. driving test
11:00 a.m.
12:00 noon dentist
1:00 p.m. appointment
2:00 p.m.
3:00 p.m. math test
4:00 p.m.
5:00 p.m.
6:00 p.m.
TUESDAY, NOVEMBER 5
8:00 a.m. hair cut!
9:00 a.m. job interview
10:00 a.m.
11:00 a.m.
12:00 noon ** vote!
1:00 p.m. Election day
2:00 p.m. baby shower
3:00 p.m.
4:00 p.m.
5:00 p.m. my son's soccer
6:00 pm. game

1. When is Maria's dentist appointment? It's on Monday at 12:00 noon.
2. How long is the math test? ....
3. What time is her haircut? ....
4. When is Election Day? ....
5. When is her son's soccer game? ....
6. How long is his soccer game? ....
7. What time is her driving test? ....
8. When is her haircut? ....
9. What time is her job interview? ....

C Read the information. Write questions with *How much, How old, What time, How long,* and *When*.

English Courses at Central Academy 1895- present					
Course	**Length of course**	**Date**	**Time**	**Cost**	**Teacher**
Grammar	1 month	October	9:00 – 11:00 daily	$500	Mr. Smith
Listening	3 weeks	November	1:00 – 3:00 daily	$400	Ms. Wood

1. Q: How long is the listening course? A: It's three weeks long.
2. Q: ....? A: It's one month long.
3. Q: ....? A: It's at 9:00 a.m.
4. Q: ....? A: It's $500.
5. Q: ....? A: It's in October
6. Q: ....? A: It's $400.
7. Q: ....? A: They're $400 and $500.
8. Q: ....? A: It's from 9:00 to 11:00.
9. Q: ....? A: It's from 1:00 to 3:00 p.m.
10. Q: ....? A: They're both two hours long.
11. Q: ....? A: The school is more than 100 years old.

D Fill in the blanks with *there, their,* or *they're.*

I have two children, a boy and a girl. Their names are David and Susan. .... very cute. David is eight years old and Susan is six years old. .... both students. .... school is near our house. .... are many students at .... school.

Have Fun

A Guessing Game Write four sentences about your family. Write three *true* sentences and one *false* sentence. Read your sentences to a small group or to your class. Your classmates will guess the sentence that is *false*.

There are ………… (number) people in my family.

They're in ………… (country) right now.

Their names are ………… (name), ………… (name), and ………… (name).

They're always very ………… (adjective).

B Unscramble the letters.

1. ………… dresses are expensive.
   h e T e s
2. ………… shoes are on sale.
   T o h s e
3. ………… is the movie?
   o w H o n l g
4. ………… girl is happy.
   h T t a
5. ………… is the table?
   o w H c h u m
6. ………… is your birthday?
   n h W e
7. ………… is your party?
   t W h a i t m e
8. ………… is a student?
   h o W

C Chant

Shopping

These shoes are nice!
How much are they?
They're not expensive.
They're on sale today.

This coat is nice.
How much is it?
It's $50.
It's a perfect fit.

That shirt is great.
Those shirts are, too.
But this is a perfect shirt for you!

Oh, look over there, that's Dora Mar.
Who's Dora Mar?
She's a movie star.

These shoes are nice.

coat

movie star

LESSON 27

Possessive Nouns

Use *'s* with nouns and names to show possession.

's with Nouns	's with Names
My **brother's** name is Gary. His **son's** name is Ronnie.	**Gary's** family is small. **Ronnie's** dog is friendly.

Language Notes

- **Incorrect:** ~~The name of my brother is Peter.~~
- In "Sue's friends are noisy," *Sue's* is possessive. *Friends* is a plural noun. The word *friends* isn't possessive, so there is no apostrophe (') before the *s* in *friends*.

A First, look at the family tree. Fill in the blanks with the names in the box below. Then listen.

Lynn (sister-in-law)	Joe (son)	Jeanne (grandmother)
Gary (brother)	Ted (uncle)	Randy (father)
Linda (daughter)	Carmen (sister)	Rachel (aunt)

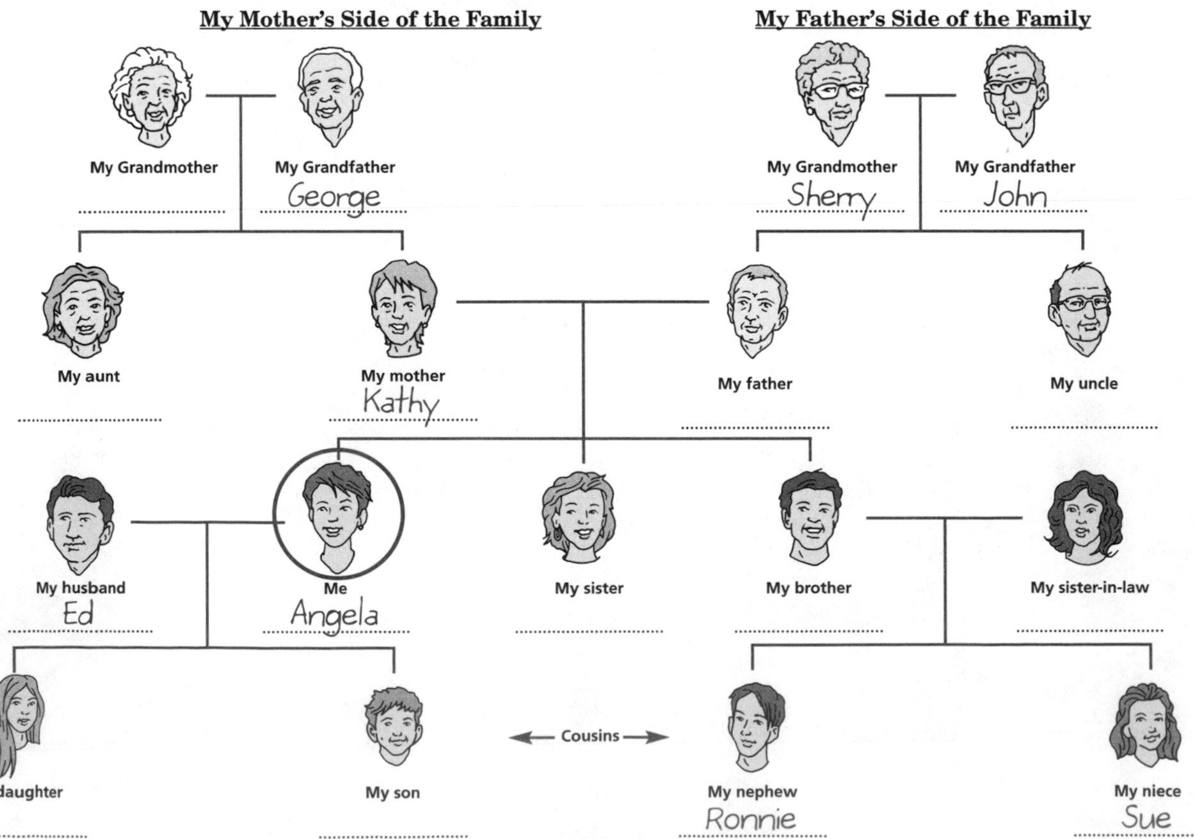

B Complete the sentences about the family in Exercise A. Use possessive nouns ('s).

Angela talks about her family. Fill in the blanks.

1. My grandmother's name is Jeanne.
2. Kathy is my ______ name.
3. My ______ name is Ed. I love him very much.
4. My ______ name is Carmen and my ______ name is Gary.
5. My ______ name is Joe and my ______ name is Linda.

Now, you talk about Angela's family. Fill in the blanks.

6. Angela is Ed's wife.
7. Joe is ______ cousin.
8. Joe is ______ brother.
9. Sue is ______ niece.
10. Ronnie is ______ nephew.

C Find the mistakes. Rewrite the sentences.

1. The desk of my daughter is messy. My daughter's desk is messy.
2. My husband car is clean. ______
3. Our dogs bed is dirty. ______
4. Our neighbors dog is friendly. ______
5. The room of Linda is big. ______
6. My son room is big, too. ______
7. My daughter's book's are on her bed. ______
8. Carmens apartment is near my house. ______

D Draw your own family tree. Use the family tree in Exercise A as a model.

- Work with a partner. Tell your partner your family members' names.
  EXAMPLE: *My mother's name is Marie.*
- Join another pair and tell them about your partner's family tree.
  EXAMPLE: *Marie is Anna's mother.*

LESSON

28 Possessive *'s*, Contracted *'s*, and Plural *s*

An *s* at the end of a noun can show different things.	
Possessive *'s*:	**Kevin's girlfriend is nice.**
Contracted *'s*:	**Kevin's a nice guy. (= Kevin is a nice guy.)**
Plural *s*:	**His friends are nice.**

AUDIO

A It's Kevin's birthday. Read the sentences about Kevin and his party. What kind of *S* is in the underlined words? Circle your answers. Then listen to the sentences.

gifts = presents

1.	Kevin's a student.	possessive *S*	(contracted *S*)	plural *S*
2.	He's 21 years old today.	possessive *S*	contracted *S*	plural *S*
3.	He's in his apartment.	possessive *S*	contracted *S*	plural *S*
4.	Kevin's happy today.	possessive *S*	contracted *S*	plural *S*
5.	Fifteen friends are at his party.	possessive *S*	contracted *S*	plural *S*
6.	Kevin's friends are nice people.	possessive *S*	contracted *S*	plural *S*
7.	There are 21 candles on his cake.	possessive *S*	contracted *S*	plural *S*
8.	Kevin's party is great.	possessive *S*	contracted *S*	plural *S*
9.	The flowers are for Kevin.	possessive *S*	contracted *S*	plural *S*
10.	And the books are for him, too.	possessive *S*	contracted *S*	plural *S*

B Fill in the blanks with *s* or *'s*.

Today is Kevin........ birthday. His friend........ are at his apartment. His parent........ aren't there. Kevin........ parent........ sent twenty-one dollar........ to Kevin. He........ very happy. And his sister........ sent him two CD........ . Kevin........ in his living room with his friend........ . They like the new CDs.

C There are five things that are wrong with this picture. Circle the things that are wrong. Then fill in the blanks with *s* or *'s*.

1. Kevin........ under the kitchen table.
2. Kevin........ two new book........ are in the refrigerator.
3. His birthday card........ are upside down.
4. The CD........ are on the wall. They aren't in the CD player.
5. Kevin........ flower........ are in a pot on the stove. They aren't in a vase.

D Chant

Betty's mother loves the mountains.

Betty's mother loves the mountains.
Betty's father loves the sea.
Betty's very happy. She loves to swim and ski.

Betty's brother Bobby loves to shop for cars.
He drives around in Hollywood, looking for the stars.

Bobby has a lot of friends. He's never all alone.
Morning, noon, and late at night, he's on his telephone.

LESSON

29 Present Tense of GO

Time Expressions

I	go	to school at 8:00 every day.
You	go	home at 2:00 every day.
He	goes	to bed at 11:00 every night.
She	goes	to the library every Saturday.
We	go	downtown every Sunday.
They	go	to the beach every summer.

Time Expressions

every day	every morning	every Sunday
every week	every afternoon	every April
every weekday	every evening	every summer
every weekend	every night	every year

Use these words with *Go*, *Go to*, and *Go to the*.

Go	Go to	Go to the
home	school	library
there	work	doctor
downtown	bed	store
downstairs	San Francisco	mall
upstairs	my friend's house	movies
inside		park
outside		mountains
		beach
		zoo

A First, read the names and the places people go. Then, listen to the sentences. Match the actions with the people.

i 1. Margaret		a. goes to work at 8:30 a.m. every weekday.
.... 2. Natasha		b. goes to school at 9:00 every morning.
.... 3. I		c. goes to bed at 10:00 every night.
.... 4. Deborah and Robin		d. go to San Francisco every week.
.... 5. Chris		e. go downtown every Saturday.
.... 6. Jack		f. go to the movies every Friday evening.
.... 7. Sharon and I		g. go to the park every weekend.
.... 8. June and Jack		h. go to the mall every Saturday.
.... 9. We		~~i.~~ goes to the store every day.

B Fill in the blanks with *go* or *goes*.

1. Margaret ......goes...... to the store every day.
2. She .... outside every day.
3. Natasha and I .... to the park every weekend.
4. My parents .... to the movies every weekend.
5. My father and mother .... to work every day.
6. I .... to the library with Natasha every month.
7. My parents .... to the beach every summer.
8. You .... to the mountains every July.
9. Jack .... to the doctor every year.
10. Natasha .... upstairs every afternoon to do her homework.

C Fill in the blanks with *go, go to,* or *go to the*.

1. We ......go to the...... mall on Sundays.
2. I .... school five days a week.
3. Every Saturday I .... park with my dad.
4. We .... home around 5:00.
5. My parents .... movies on Friday nights.
6. I .... my friend's house every afternoon.

D Fill in the blanks with *goes, goes to,* or *goes to the*.

1. Natasha ......goes to...... school at 9:00 a.m.
2. She .... home at 5:00.
3. She .... bed at 11:00.
4. My mother .... San Francisco on Sundays.
5. My father .... library on Saturday mornings.
6. He .... park with me on Saturdays.

E Write nine sentences about where you and other people go on different days.

Sentences 1-3: You
Sentences 4-6: A friend or someone in your family
Sentences 7-9: Two friends or two people in your family

EXAMPLE: I go downtown on Saturdays. I go to the park every Sunday.
I go to school on weekdays from 9:00 to 3:30.

LESSON

30 Present Tense of GO + Activities (*go* ___*ing*)

verb

Prepositions, Seasons, and Days

Use *go* ___*ing* to talk about an activity. Use *go to* to talk about where you do the activity.

		Activity			Place
I	go	shopping every Saturday.	I	go	to the store.
You	go	dancing every Saturday night.	You	go	to a club.
He	goes	swimming on Sundays.	He	goes	to a swimming pool.
She	goes	skiing every winter.	She	goes	to the mountains.
We	go	fishing in the summer.	We	go	to a lake.
They	go	bike-riding every weekend.	They	go	to a park.
		jogging			to a park.
		ice-skating			to a skating rink.
		sightseeing			to a new place.

Language Notes

- **Incorrect**: go ~~to~~ shopping
- **Seasons**: summer, fall (autumn), winter, spring
- **Prepositions** with seasons and days:

I go swimming **in the summer**. = I go swimming **every** summer.
He goes swimming **on Sundays**. = He goes swimming **every** Sunday.

A Look at the pictures and read the words. Listen to the sentences about Elena and Mario. Write the season (*summer, fall, winter, spring*) under each activity.

1. 

go jogging

summer

2. 

go swimming

....

3. 

go shopping

....

4. 

go skiing

....

5. 

go bike-riding

....

6. 

go ice-skating

....

B Elena and Mario have three busy children—Roberto (R), Susie (S), and Marta (M). Look at their after-school activities on Mondays, Wednesdays, and Fridays. Then complete the sentences.

Mondays	**Wednesdays**	**Fridays**
M and S: ice-skating	R: bowling	M and S: bike-riding
	S: swimming	R: bowling
R: bike-riding	M: ice-skating	

1. On Mondays, Roberto goes bike-riding.
2. On Mondays, Susie and Marta ______________.
3. On Wednesdays and Fridays, Roberto ______________.
4. On Wednesdays, Susie ______________.
5. On Wednesdays, Marta ______________.
6. On Fridays, Susie and Marta ______________.

C Follow steps 1, 2, and 3.

Step 1: Write two things you do every week.

EXAMPLE: I go shopping on Mondays.

OR I go shopping every Monday.

____

____

Step 2: Work with a partner. Read your sentences from Step 1 to each other. Then write two things your partner does every week.

EXAMPLE: Jose goes fishing every Wednesday.

OR Jose goes fishing on Wednesdays.

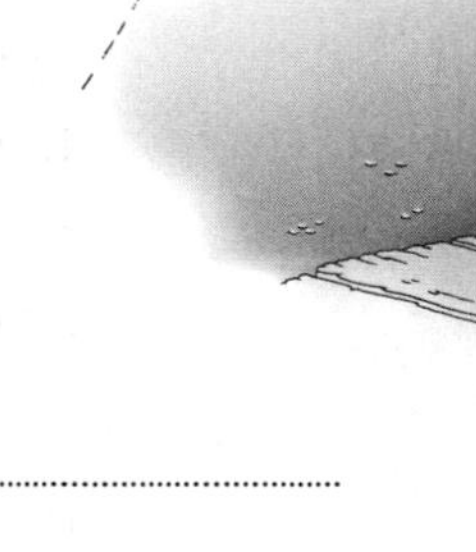

____

____

Step 3: Join another pair. Tell the other students what your partner does every week.

Lessons 27–30

Review

Possessive Nouns, Expressions with *go*, and *'s* vs. *s*

A Dictation Listen to the sentences about a family's routine. Write what you hear. Key words: *daughter, husband, bike-riding, Wednesdays.*

1. Every day ____________
2. ____________
3. ____________
4. ____________

B Write three sentences with *go* or *goes* about people you know. Write one sentence about you. Use the sentences in Exercise A as models.

EXAMPLE: Every day my roommate goes to work at 7:00 a.m.

1. Every day ____________.
2. ____________.
3. ____________ every Saturday.
4. I ____________ on Wednesdays.

C Write the words in the correct column.

downtown	doctor	outside
home	mall	sightseeing
library	work	bed
mountains	Tim's house	Mexico
school	swimming	beach

GO	GO TO	GO TO THE
downtown		

D Find the mistakes. Rewrite the sentences.

1. My mother name is Susan. — My mother's name is Susan.
2. My brother go to school every day. — ....
3. This is my teacher book. — ....
4. The children goes to bed early. — ....
5. I go to home at 5:00 p.m. — ....
6. I have three children, two boy's and a girl. — ....
7. I go to shopping on Saturdays. — ....
8. I'm go to work at 8:00. — ....
9. My teacher name is Charlie. — ....
10. I go school at 7:45. — ....
11. She's go to the store every Sunday. — ....
12. You go to the Mexico every year. — ....

E Read the paragraph, "My Saturdays." Then write the paragraph again, but change *I* to *she* and *my* to *her*. Change the verbs, too. Use the present tense.

My Saturdays

I am very busy on Saturdays. Every Saturday morning, I go to the gym. After that, I go shopping. I go to the supermarket and the farmer's market. Sometimes on Saturday afternoons, I go to my friend's house. On Saturday evenings, I go to the movies, or I go dancing with my friends.

Kelly's Saturdays

Kelly is very busy on weekends. Every Saturday morning, she ....

....

....

....

....

....

....

Have Fun

A Word Search Write *go, go to,* or *go to the* in front of the words below. Then circle the words in the puzzle. The words can be vertical (|), horizontal (—), or diagonal (/). The words can also be spelled backwards.

1.	go to the	beach	**8.**	....	library
2.	....	bed	**9.**	....	work
3.	....	dancing	**10.**	....	movies
4.	....	there	**11.**	....	school
5.	....	doctor	**12.**	....	upstairs
6.	....	downtown	**13.**	....	shopping
7.	....	home	**14.**	....	swimming

M	O	V	I	E	S	D	H	R	S	L	U	T	G	Y
L	E	W	F	W	D	C	L	H	H	O	M	E	U	G
I	U	I	Z	H	R	T	O	B	E	D	P	X	N	A
B	K	G	A	U	G	P	S	W	I	M	M	I	N	G
R	I	R	H	R	P	C	U	O	T	S	C	D	U	K
A	D	C	T	I	S	Z	A	D	S	N	B	O	B	U
R	O	V	N	H	I	P	R	J	A	X	P	C	U	P
Y	W	G	S	U	E	N	P	D	T	K	P	T	H	S
R	N	P	G	K	D	R	Z	D	R	S	O	O	Y	T
M	T	G	E	L	P	I	E	O	C	O	E	R	O	A
B	O	X	I	H	Y	F	W	W	T	Y	H	L	O	I
V	W	V	Y	V	S	C	H	O	O	L	O	U	K	R
O	N	T	I	B	E	A	C	H	I	T	M	A	Q	S

B Chant

Summer Days, Summer Nights

Nick goes to bed every night at eleven.
His Grandma goes to bed at seven.
His sister Sue goes to bed at eight.
But his Mom and Dad go to bed very late.

Nick goes swimming with his sister Sue.
They go to the pool every day at two.
On summer nights they go for a walk
With their Mom and Dad and laugh and talk.

Sometimes Grandma goes to the mall.
She doesn't go to the pool at all.
She loves to go shopping with her old friend Joan.
She never goes to the mall alone.

LESSON

31 Present Tense—Affirmative Statements

Time Expressions

Use the present tense to talk about something that *repeats* or is *routine*.

- Use the base form of the verb with *I, you, we, they.*
- For most verbs, use the base form + *s* with *he, she, it.*

Subject	Verb	When/How Often	
I You We They	work	every day every morning every evening every night	every week every month every year
He She It	works	once a week (= one time every week) twice a week (= two times every week) three times a week	

Language Notes:
S Spelling: When a verb ends in *sh* or *ch*, add *es*: brush-brushes watch-watches
Special Spelling: go-goes do-does

A Look at the pictures. They are not in the correct order. Listen to the information about Sandy. Number the pictures in the correct order.

A. Sandy wakes up at 6:00 every morning.

B. At 7:30, she goes to work.

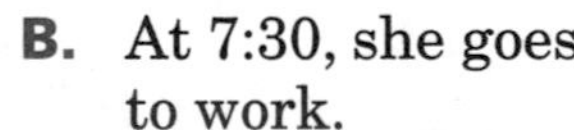

C. She eats breakfast.

1 ....

....

....

D. She brushes her teeth.

E. She gets up at 6:15.

F. She takes a shower.

....

....

....

B Sandy talks about her morning, and her husband Andy talks about her. Fill in the blanks with the verbs from Exercise A.

1. Sandy: I ......wake up...... at 6:00 every morning.
   Andy: Sandy ......wakes up...... at 6:00 every morning.
2. Sandy: I .... at 6:15.
   Andy: She .... at 6:15.
3. Sandy: Then I .... my teeth.
   Andy: Then she .... her teeth.
4. Sandy: After that, I .... a shower.
   Andy: After that, she .... a shower.
5. Sandy: I .... breakfast.
   Andy: She .... breakfast.
6. Sandy: I .... to work at 7:30.
   Andy: She .... to work at 7:30.

Correct:
"eat breakfast" or
"have breakfast"

Incorrect:
"~~take~~ breakfast"

C Complete the sentences about the things that Sandy and Andy do. (Different answers are possible.)

Use these verbs: go eat out go dancing call ride eat

Use these time expressions: at 10:00 on Saturdays once a week twice a month every evening

1. We ...eat... dinner together ...every evening... .
2. We .... to bed ....
3. We .... our bikes ....
4. We .... our grandchildren ....
5. We ....

What do Sandy and Andy do?

6. They ...eat... dinner together ...every evening... .
7. They ....
8. They ....
9. They ....
10. They ....

D Write five sentences about what you do (1) every morning, (2) every afternoon, (3) every evening, (4) every Saturday, and (5) every Sunday. Read your sentences to your partner. Then write five sentences about your partner.

LESSON

32 Present Tense—Spelling

Reminder
C = Consonant
(b, c, d, f, g, h, j, k, l, m, n, p, q, r, s, t, v, w, x, y, z)

V = Vowel
(a, e, i, o, u)

Use the base form of the verb with *I, you, we,* and *they.*

With *he, she,* or *it,* use these rules:

1. **Add *s* to most verbs.**

   work-works **make-makes** **play-plays**

2. **Add *es* to verbs that end in *ch, sh, s,* or *x.***

   watch-watches **brush-brushes** **miss-misses** **fix-fixes**

3. **When a verb ends in a consonant (C) + *y,* drop the *y* and add *ies.***

   trу-tries **carrу-carries**

   Be careful: When a verb ends in a vowel (V) + *y,* just add *s.*

   play-plays

4. **Special Spelling: go-goes do-does**

A Listen to the paragraphs about Sandy and her husband, Andy. After you listen, underline the verbs. Then write the number of the spelling rule for each verb.

Sandy lives in New York with her husband Andy. Every morning, Sandy gets up early and goes to work. She works in the city at a software company. She takes her laptop computer to work every day. Sometimes she plays computer games on the train when she goes to work.

Andy works at home. He writes computer programs. He gets up around 9:00 a.m. After he brushes his teeth, he makes breakfast and watches TV. He tries to work eight hours a day, but sometimes he works six or ten hours. When he takes a break, he plays the guitar.

Verbs	Rule Numbers	Verbs	Rule Numbers	Verbs	Rule Numbers
lives	1	takes	....	makes	....
gets up	....	plays	....	watches	....
goes	....	writes	....	tries	....
works	....	brushes	....		

B Write the he/she form of the verb on the lines.

He/She . . .

1. wake up ......wakes up......
2. get up ....
3. get out of bed ....
4. brush her teeth ....
5. wash her face ....
6. take a shower ....
7. wash her hair ....
8. get dressed ....
9. eat breakfast ....
10. drink coffee ....
11. go to work ....
12. take the train ....
13. miss the bus ....
14. stay home ....
15. walk the dog ....
16. make dinner ....
17. study English ....
18. fix computers ....

get up

get dressed

take the train

miss the bus

walk the dog

fix computers

C Work with a partner. Ask your partner the questions below and take notes. Then, on a separate piece of paper, write sentences about your partner and share them with the class.

EXAMPLE: Note—*7:00*
Sentence—*Yolanda gets up at 7:00.*

My partner: ....
(your partner's first name)

Questions	**Notes**
1. What time do you get up?	....
2. What do you do first?	....
3. What do you do after that?	....
4. What do you do next?	....
5. Then what do you do?	....
6. What do you do after that?	....

LESSON

33 Present Tense of *Do, Have, Make,* and *Take*—Affirmative Statements

With *I, you, we, they:* Use the base form of the verb.
With *he, she, it* : Use *has* or use the base form of the verb + *s* or *es.*

	Have	**Do**	**Make**	**Take**
I, You, We, They	**have**	**do**	**make**	**take**
He, She, It	**has**	**does**	**makes**	**takes**

Phrases with these verbs:

Have

have a good time = have fun
have a snack
have breakfast/lunch/dinner
Incorrect: ~~take~~ breakfast

Do

do my homework
Incorrect: ~~make~~ my homework
do laundry; do *the* laundry; do *my* laundry
do the dishes

Make

make breakfast/lunch/dinner
make the bed; make *my* bed
make a mistake/make mistakes
make a phone call

Take

take a test
Incorrect: ~~make~~ a test
take a bus; take *the* bus
take a break
take a nap
take a walk
take care of

A Look at the pictures of Sandy's husband, Andy. Listen to the sentences. Write the number of the sentence that goes with each picture.

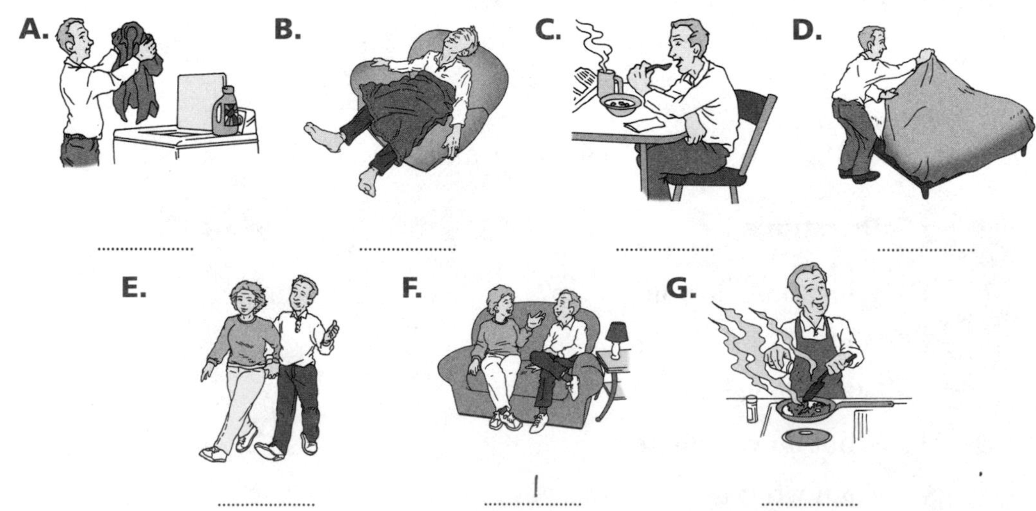

B Fill in the blanks with the correct form of *do, have, make* or *take*.

1. Andy ......has...... breakfast around 9:30.
2. Sandy .... breakfast at 7:00 a.m.
3. They .... dinner at 7:00 p.m.
4. Andy .... the bed in the morning.
5. Sandy .... the train to work.
6. Andy .... the laundry.
7. Sandy and Andy .... a walk in the evening.
8. Their grandson is eight. He .... his homework every night.
9. Their grandson .... mistakes in math.
10. He .... tests every week.
11. His friends .... tests every week, too.
12. He .... care of his little sister.

C Ask your classmates these questions. Write their first names in the circles IF they say "Yes." Write at least two names for each question.

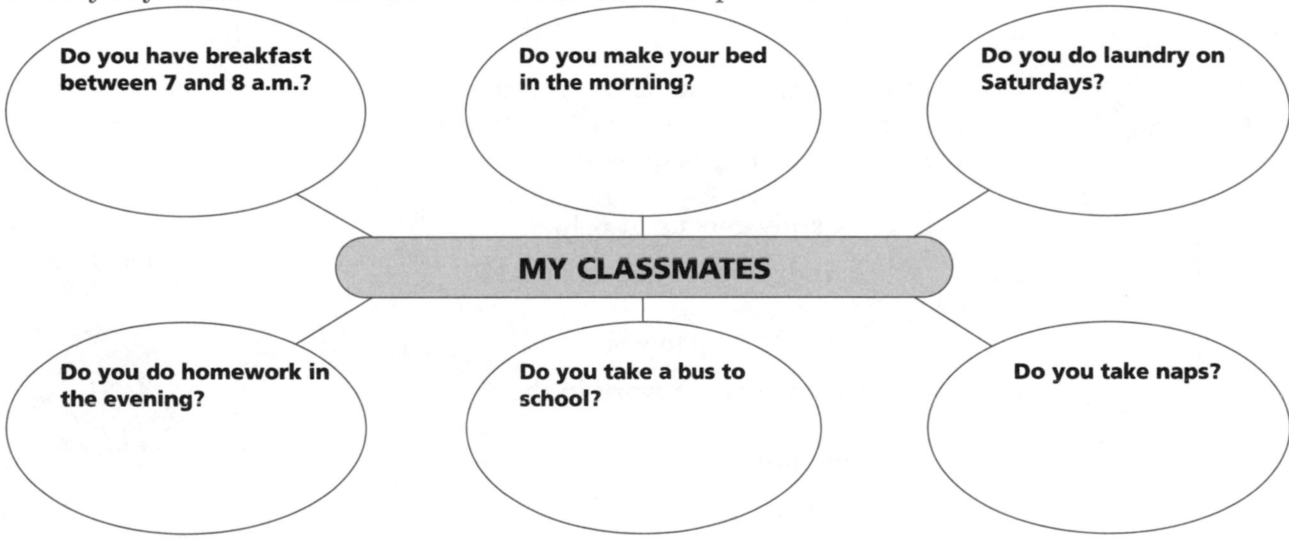

Do you have breakfast between 7 and 8 a.m.?
Do you make your bed in the morning?
Do you do laundry on Saturdays?
MY CLASSMATES
Do you do homework in the evening?
Do you take a bus to school?
Do you take naps?

Write ten sentences about your classmates.

EXAMPLE: *Patricia and Rika have breakfast between 7:00 and 8:00 a.m.*

AUDIO

D Chant

A Good Life

He makes breakfast.
She makes the bed.
They do the dishes.
She makes the bread.

He does the laundry.
She irons his pants.
He takes care of
their beautiful plants.

He makes the coffee.
She makes the tea.
They take vacations
By the sea.

LESSON 34

Present Tense—Negative Statements

Do is a *helping verb.* Use *do* with *not* to make a negative statement in the present tense.

Affirmative Statements		Negative Statements		
Subject	**Verb**	**Subject**	**Helping Verb**	**Main Verb**
I	work.	I	don't	work.
You	work.	You	don't	work.
We	work.	We	don't	work.
They	work.	They	don't	work.
He	works.	He	doesn't	work.*
She	works.	She	doesn't	work.*
It	works.	It	doesn't	work.*

*When you use *doesn't,* always use the base form of the main verb. Do not add an *s.*

A Read these sentences about Sandy and Andy. Underline the verbs. Write **A** if the sentence is affirmative, and **N** if the sentence is negative. Listen to the sentences. Then practice reading the sentences with a partner.

1. A Sandy gets up at 6:15.
   N Andy doesn't get up at 6:15.
2. ______ Sandy goes to work in the city.
   ______ Andy doesn't work in the city.
3. ______ Sandy plays computer games.
   ______ Andy plays the guitar.
4. ______ Sandy doesn't make dinner.
   ______ Andy makes dinner.
5. ______ They don't go to restaurants a lot.
   ______ Andy is a good cook.
6. ______ They don't go to the movies a lot.
   ______ They read newspapers and magazines and watch TV.
7. ______ They don't go to bed very late.
   ______ They go to bed around 10:00.

B Write negative sentences about Andy.

	Affirmative sentences	Negative sentences	
1.	Andy works at home.	He doesn't work	in the city.
2.	He writes computer programs.	....	books.
3.	He gets up around 9:00 a.m.	....	at 7:00 a.m.
4.	He takes a break in the afternoon.	....	a break in the morning.
5.	He plays the guitar.	....	the piano.
6.	He does the laundry on Wednesdays.	....	the laundry on Thursdays.

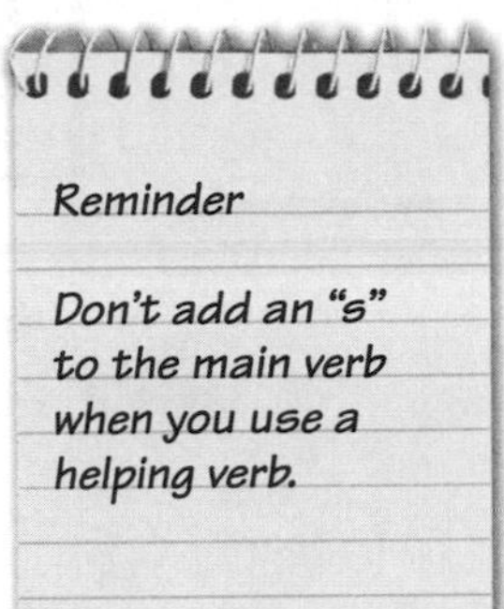

Reminder
Don't add an "s" to the main verb when you use a helping verb.

C Write negative sentences about Andy and Sandy.

1. Andy and Sandy use computers. They don't use typewriters.
2. They work with computers. .... with typewriters.
3. They have dinner at 7:00. .... dinner at 9:00.
4. They watch TV in the evening. .... TV in the afternoon.
5. They talk during dinner. .... during lunch.
6. They take a walk after dinner. .... a walk after lunch.

D Write negative sentences.

1. I (have) don't have breakfast at 10:00 a.m.
2. You (have) .... lunch at 3:00 p.m.
3. He (have) .... dinner at 9:00 p.m.
4. We (have) .... a snack at 11:00 p.m.
5. They (have) .... a good time at work.
6. She (do) .... laundry once a week.
7. He (do) .... laundry twice a week.
8. They (do) .... laundry three times a week.
9. I (do) .... my homework in the afternoon.
10. You (make) .... your bed.
11. We (make) .... mistakes a lot.
12. She (make) .... a lot of mistakes.
13. They (take) .... tests every week.
14. I (take) .... the bus to school.
15. You (take) .... a break in the morning.
16. He (take) .... a nap every day.
17. It (rain) .... in the summer.
18. It (sleep) .... in the house.

Lessons 31–34

Review
Present Tense

A Dictation Listen to the sentences about a lazy teenager. Write what you hear. Key words: *lazy, laundry.*

1. Sometimes ____________
2. ____________
3. ____________
4. ____________
5. ____________

B These verbs have different *s* forms. Put the verbs in the correct list in the chart.

brush	go	play	wake	carry	try
~~get~~	stay	walk	do	make	work
study	wash	fix	miss	take	watch

-s	-es	-ies
gets		

C Use some of the verbs from Exercise B in these sentences. You can use the verbs more than once.

1. Every morning, my brother __washes__ his face, ________ his teeth, and ________ dressed.
2. He ________ the bus to school. Sometimes he ________ up late, and he ________ the bus.
3. He ________ hard at school. After school, he ________ soccer.

4. When he .... home, he .... the dog and .... the guitar.

5. After dinner, he .... his homework.

6. He .... a shower at 9:00 p.m. and he .... to bed at 10:00 pm.

D Complete the chart.

		Singular	Plural
1.	Affirmative:	He plays soccer.	They play soccer.
	Negative:	He doesn't play soccer.	They don't play soccer.
2.	Affirmative:	She goes to school.	We ....
	Negative:	She	We ....
3.	Affirmative:	She	They study English.
	Negative:	She	They ....
4.	Affirmative:	He	We ....
	Negative:	He doesn't do the laundry.	We ....
5.	Affirmative:	She	They ....
	Negative:	She	They don't have breakfast.

E Find the mistakes. Rewrite the sentences.

1. I no have a job. I don't have a job.
2. This class have many students. ....
3. My friend no like this city. ....
4. My husband work in New York. ....
5. I'm call my family every week. ....
6. My country have beautiful weather. ....
7. He studys hard. ....
8. He washes the dishes. ....
9. He plaies soccer. ....
10. I make my homework every day. ....
11. We make a test every Friday. ....

LESSONS 31–34

Have Fun

A Crossword Puzzle

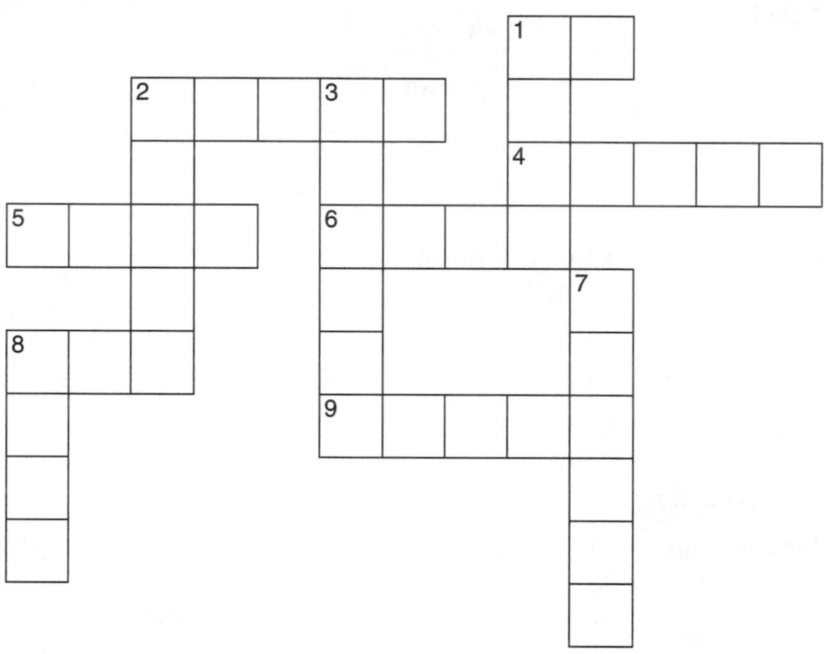

Across

1. We .... to school twice a week.
2. We .... English at school.
4. She .... to her sister on the phone every day.
5. The children .... soccer after school.
6. David's father .... breakfast at 7:00.
8. My brother .... three children, two boys and a girl.
9. My daughter .... the bus to school.

Down

1. He .... up at 9:00 every morning.
2. My daughter .... home when she is sick.
3. My son is lazy. He .... work hard.
7. When he wakes up late, he .... the bus.
8. We .... a good time in our class.

B Guessing Game Write three sentences about yourself. Write two *true* sentences and one *false* sentence. Read your sentences to a small group or to your class. Your classmates will guess the sentence that is *false*. Use the simple present tense.

EXAMPLE: I have four brothers. I work in a bank. I speak French.

Your classmates can say: You don't work in a bank. You work in a hotel.

C Chant

Jack loves Jill.

Jack lives in San Francisco.
His girlfriend's in L.A.
He calls her on her birthday.
He sends her flowers in May.

Jack plays in a jazz band.
His girlfriend plays the guitar.
Jack takes a cable car to work.
His girlfriend drives her car.

Jack works very late at night.
His girlfriend works all day.
But every Saturday morning
He flies down to L.A.

LESSON

35 Present Tense—Yes-No Questions and Short Answers

Do and *does* are "helping verbs." They help make questions.

Statement:		They	go to school.
Yes-No Question:	Do	they	go to school?

Questions	Short Answers		Other Answers
Do I have homework?	Yes, you do.	No, you don't.	I don't know.
Do you like school?	Yes, I do.	No, I don't.	Sure.
Does he go to school?*	Yes, he does.	No, he doesn't.	Uh-huh. (= yes)
Does she teach math?*	Yes, she does.	No, she doesn't.	Uh-uh. (=no)
Does it rain in November?*	Yes, it does.	No, it doesn't.	
Do we work hard?	Yes, we do.	No, we don't.	
Do you like school?	Yes, we do.	No, we don't.	
Do they want pizza?	Yes, they do.	No, they don't.	I don't know.

*When you use *does*, always use the base form of the main verb. Do not add an *s*.

A Look at the picture and read the questions. Listen to the conversation. Then read the questions again and circle *Yes, No,* or *I don't know.*

1.	Does Ben want to take a walk?	(Yes, he does.)	No, he doesn't.	I don't know.
2.	Does Robbie go to school?	Yes, he does.	No, he doesn't.	I don't know.
3.	Does Robbie like science?	Yes, he does.	No, he doesn't.	I don't know.
4.	Does Ben teach math?	Yes, he does.	No, he doesn't.	I don't know.
5.	Does Ben teach third grade?	Yes, he does.	No, he doesn't.	I don't know.
6.	Does Ben's wife teach high school?	Yes, she does.	No, she doesn't.	I don't know.
7.	Does Ben's wife like teaching?	Yes, she does.	No, she doesn't.	I don't know.
8.	Do Andy and Robbie take a walk every day?	Yes, they do.	No, they don't.	I don't know.

B Ask Robbie questions. Then ask Andy questions about Robbie. Use the verbs in parentheses.

Questions for Robbie:	Questions for Andy:
1. You: (like) Do you like school? Robbie: Yes, I do.	You: (like) Does he like school? Andy: Yes, he does.
2. You: (study) .... a lot? Robbie: Yes, I do.	You: (study) .... a lot? Andy: Yes, he does.
3. You: (do) .... homework every weeknight? Robbie: Yes, I do.	You: (do) .... homework every weeknight? Andy: Yes, he does.
4. You: (do) .... homework on Saturday nights? Robbie: No, I don't.	You: (do) .... homework on Saturday nights? Andy: No, he doesn't.

C Write *true* answers to the questions under *About You*. Then ask your partner the same questions and write his or her answers.

EXAMPLE: Do you like ice cream? No, I don't. Yes, she does.

	About You	About Your Classmate
1. Do you have a brother?	....	....
2. Do you have a sister?	....	....
3. Do you have a job?	....	....
4. Do you and your friends like movies?	....	....
5. Does it rain a lot in your city or town?	....	....

"Brothers" are boys and men only, not girls or women.

D Chant

Do you like movies?

Do you like movies?
Yes, I do.
I love movies.
I do, too.

Do your friends like movies?
Yes, they do.
They love movies.
My friends do, too.

Do you travel a lot?
Yes, I do.
I love to travel.
I do, too.

Do you study a lot?
Yes, I do.
I study English.
I do too.

LESSON

36 Present Tense with Frequency Adverbs

Always, Usually, Often, Sometimes, Rarely, *and* Never

Use *always, usually, often, sometimes, rarely,* and *never* to talk about how often something happens. Put these words AFTER the verb *BE*. Put them BEFORE other verbs.

Subject		**Verb**	
I	always	exercise	three times a week.
You	usually	go	jogging every day.
We	often	go	swimming in the summer.
They	sometimes	play	tennis on Saturdays.
He/She	rarely	play<u>s</u>	baseball in the winter.
It	never	rain<u>s</u>	in the summer.

Always — 100%
Usually
Often
Sometimes — 50%
Rarely
Never — 0%

Subject	***BE***		
I	am	always	busy.

Language Notes

- ***Sometimes*** **can be in three places:**
  They *sometimes* play tennis. *Sometimes* they play tennis. They play tennis *sometimes*.

See Lesson 8 for *BE* with frequency adverbs.

A Simona and Jon are high school students. They are athletes. They play sports a lot. Listen to the conversation and fill in the blanks with *always, usually, often, sometimes, rarely,* or *never*.

1. Hi. I'm Simona. I love sports, and I ....always.... exercise every day.
2. Hello. My name's Jon. I love sports too, but I don't exercise every day. I .... exercise around three times a week.
3. We watch sports on TV a lot. We .... watch one or two games every day.
4. I .... go jogging in the afternoon.
5. I .... go jogging. I like swimming.
6. Jon, that's not true. You .... go jogging.
7. I .... go jogging.
8. Well, we're .... busy, that's for sure!

B Write the verbs and frequency adverbs from Exercise A below. Circle *before* if the adverb comes before the verb. Circle *after* if it comes after the verb *be*.

1. always exercise .... (before) after
2. .... before after
3. .... before after
4. .... before after
5. .... before after
6. .... before after
7. .... before after
8. .... before after

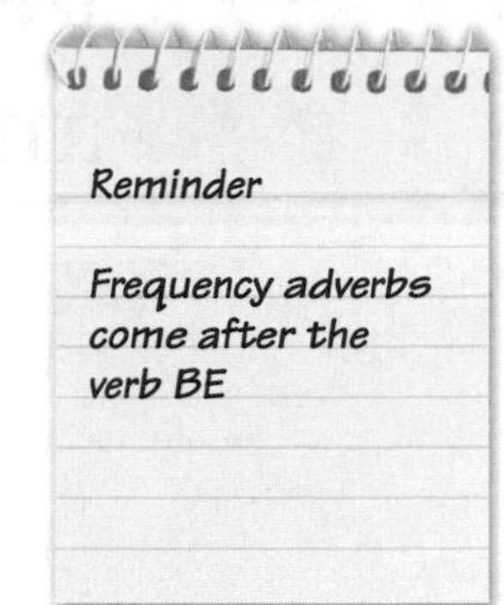

Reminder
Frequency adverbs come after the verb BE

C This is a typical month for Simona. Complete the sentences with *always, usually, often, sometimes, rarely*, or *never* + a verb.

SUNDAY	MONDAY	TUESDAY	WEDNESDAY	THURSDAY	FRIDAY	SATURDAY
work at sports center	watch football	go swimming 5 p.m.		go jogging 3:30		8 a.m. play tennis
work			go swimming 5 p.m.	go jogging 3:30	go to the movies 7:00 p.m.	8 a.m. play tennis go shopping
work	watch football	go swimming 5 p.m.		go jogging 3:30		10 a.m. play volleyball
2 p.m. soccer game				go jogging 3:30	movies 7 p.m.	8 a.m. play tennis

1. Simona always goes jogging on Thursday afternoons.
2. She .... swimming on Tuesdays.
3. She .... swimming on Mondays.
4. She .... volleyball on Thursdays.
5. She .... at the sports center on Sundays.
6. She .... football on Monday nights.
7. She .... plays football on Friday nights.
8. She .... tennis on Saturday mornings.

D Make your own calendar for a typical month. Write sentences about yourself. Use the simple present tense with frequency adverbs. Then work with a partner. Look at your partner's calendar, and write sentences about your partner.

LESSON

37 Present Tense of *Want*, *Need*, *Like*, and *Have* + Infinitives

An infinitive is *to* + the base form of a verb. Use infinitives after *want, need, like,* and *have*.

Affirmative	**Negative**
I **want to have** a big wedding.	I **don't want to have** a small wedding.
He **needs to wear** a tuxedo.	He **doesn't need to wear** a hat.
We **like to dance**.	We **don't like to sit** at a party.
She **has to buy** a wedding gown.	She **doesn't have to buy** shoes.

Language Notes

Use the base form of the verb after *to*. Don't add an *s*.

Correct: She has to **buy** a wedding gown.

Incorrect: She has to **buys** a wedding gown.

A Judy and Brian are planning their wedding. Look at the pictures. They are not in the correct order. Listen and number the pictures in the correct order.

A.

....

B.

....

C.

....

D.

1

E.

....

F.

....

B Fill in the blanks. Write the opposite.

1. We *don't want to have* a small wedding.
   We ...want to have... a big wedding.
2. They *don't need to buy* a birthday cake.
   They .... a wedding cake.
3. Judy's dad *likes to take* pictures.
   Judy's mom .... pictures.
4. Brian *doesn't need to get* a haircut.
   Judy .... a haircut.
5. Brian's parents *don't have to pay*.
   Judy's parents ....
6. They *want to have* a wonderful day.
   They .... problems.

C What do you like/want/need/have to do? What don't you like/want/need/have to do? Complete the chart with the verbs in the list. You can use the words more than one time.

go shopping	eat out	do laundry	make my bed
go swimming	eat outside	go swimming	go to the bank
talk to my friends	cook	use a computer	sing
take naps	sleep	have a good time	dance
take walks	go to sleep late	clean my room	speak English
do my homework	sleep late	go home	go to work

I like to:	**I want to:**	**I need to:**	**I have to:**
I don't like to:	**I don't want to:**	**I don't need to:**	**I don't have to:**

D Use the chart in Exercise C. Write four sentences about yourself (two affirmative and two negative) on a separate piece of paper. Read your sentences to a partner. Then write four sentences about your partner.

LESSON

38 Present Tense—Questions with *What/Where/When/Why/Who*

Use *what, where, when, why,* or *who* to ask for information.

WH-Question Word	Helping Verb	Subject	Main Verb*	
What	do	you	eat	for breakfast?
What	does	he	eat	for breakfast?
Where	do	they	go	on weekends?
Where	does	she	go	on weekends?
When	do	you	take	a break?
When	does	he	take	a break?
Why	do	you	take	classes?
Why	does	he	take	classes?
Who	do	you	live	with?
Who	does	she	live	with?
What time	do	we	start?	
What time	does	it (the movie)	start?	

*In a question, always use the base form of the main verb. Do not add an *s*.

A Donna, a student, is answering questions at her school. Listen and circle the answers that you hear.

	Questions	Answers	
1.	What time do you get up?	At 7:00.	At 8:00.
2.	What do you eat for breakfast?	Cereal.	Toast.
3.	Who do you live with?	My parents.	My sister.
4.	What time does school start?	At 8:10.	At 9:10.
5.	Does your school have good classes?	Yes, it does.	No, it doesn't.
6.	What do you do on weekends?	I relax.	I study and work.
7.	Do you have free time on weekends?	Yes, a little.	No.
8.	When do you do your homework?	In the evening.	In the afternoon.
9.	Where do you go to school?	In the city.	In my neighborhood.
10.	Why do you go to school?	I want a good job.	I want to be a doctor.

B Write the words in the correct order to make questions. There are four Yes-No questions and eight Wh questions.

1. time/What/up/you/do/get .... What time do you get up?
2. breakfast/eat/you/Do ....
3. breakfast/eat/you/do/What/for ....
4. work/you/Do ....
5. English/you/study/Why/do ....
6. to/go/you/school/Do ....
7. study/do/What/you ....
8. home/go/you/When/do ....
9. dinner/Do/make/you ....
10. time/have/you/What/dinner/do ....
11. Who/with/dinner/you/do/have ....
12. homework/Where/you/do/do/your ....

C Follow the steps below.

- Write six questions from Exercise B in the chart.
- Write two more questions.
- Ask a partner the questions. Write his or her short answers.

EXAMPLE: What time do you get up? At 7:00. At 7:30.

Questions	Your Partner's Short Answers
1.	....
2.	....
3.	....
4.	....
5.	....
6.	....
7.	....
8.	....

Now write eight sentences about your partner on a separate piece of paper.

EXAMPLE: Donna gets up at 7:00.

Lessons 35–38

Review

Present Tense

A Dictation Two students are talking after class. Listen to their conversation and write what you hear. Key words: *weekends, movies.*

A: What do ....

B: ....

A: ....

B: ....

B Write *Do* or *Does*. Then write *true* short answers.

1. Do you live in the U.S.? Yes, I do.
2. ...... your teacher give a lot of homework? ....
3. ...... this school have a computer lab? ....
4. ...... the students in this class study hard? ....
5. ...... these exercises help you learn grammar? ....
6. ...... this classroom have a TV? ....
7. ...... you like to do grammar exercises? ....
8. ...... your teacher speak your first language? ....

C Rewrite the sentences with *always, usually, often, sometimes, rarely*, or *never*. Write *true* sentences.

1. I speak English at home. I rarely speak English at home.
2. I do my homework. ....
3. I am late for class. ....
4. I am absent from class. ....
5. I watch sports on TV. ....
6. I go to the movies on weekends. ....
7. I'm homesick. ....
8. I play soccer after work. ....
9. I'm happy. ....
10. I lose my keys. ....

D Find the mistakes. Rewrite the sentences.

1. I like study English. .... I like to study English.
2. What time he go to school? ....
3. Does your sister lives in the U.S.? ....
4. Where you live? ....
5. What time your class begin? ....
6. I want study English. ....
7. My husband needs work hard. ....
8. When you go to work? ....
9. Does your father speaks English? ....
10. She have to work after school. ....

E Write questions for the answers.

1. A: Where do you live?
   B: I live in San Francisco.
2. A: ....?
   B: My parents live in Mexico.
3. A: ....?
   B: I work at a bank.
4. A: ....?
   B: My husband works in a restaurant.
5. A: .... children?
   B: Yes, I have one son.
6. A: ....?
   B: He's five years old.
7. A: ....?
   B: My class starts at 10:00 a.m.
8. A: ....?
   B: My class ends at noon.

Have Fun

A Word Search Write the words in the chart. Then circle the words in the puzzle. The words can be vertical (|), horizontal (—), or diagonal (/). The words can also be spelled backwards.

always	**homework**	**class**
dinner	**make**	**rarely**
football	**need**	**sometimes**
guitar	**never**	**take**
have	**often**	**want**

Adverbs of Frequency	Nouns	Verbs
always		

W	K	M	A	K	E	P	F	T	L
A	I	R	A	L	W	A	Y	S	L
N	O	R	O	O	F	T	E	N	A
T	V	N	A	W	F	I	N	M	B
W	R	L	D	R	E	E	D	U	T
S	E	M	I	T	E	M	O	S	O
S	V	T	N	D	C	L	O	W	O
A	E	A	N	A	W	S	Y	H	F
L	N	K	E	R	A	T	I	U	G
C	O	E	R	E	V	A	H	I	C

B Chant

Does she like to cook?

Does she like to cook?
No, she doesn't.
She loves to eat,
But she doesn't like to cook.

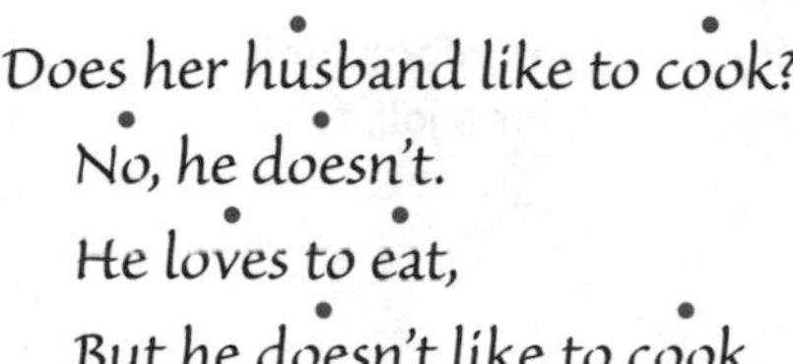

Does her husband like to cook?
No, he doesn't.
He loves to eat,
But he doesn't like to cook.

Where do they have dinner?
On Maple Street,
In a Spanish restaurant
With great things to eat.

When do they have dinner?
Usually at eight.
Sometimes they're early,
But they're never late.

LESSON 39

Present Continuous Tense—Affirmative Statements

Use the present continuous tense to talk about what is happening RIGHT NOW.
The present continuous tense has two parts: *BE* and verb + *ing*.

	PART 1 *BE*	PART 2 verb + *ing*	
I	am	looking	for a job at a job fair.
You	are	listening	to Paula.
He	is	wearing	blue jeans.
She	is	reading	information.
It	is	raining.	
We	are	looking	at information.
They	are	looking	for a job, too.

A Look at the picture of a job fair in a high school gym. Read the sentences. Then listen to the TV reporter. Write *T* for *True* or *F* for *False* on the lines.

Right now:

T 1. The TV reporter is at a job fair.

____ 2. The job fair is outside.

____ 3. The reporter is talking to people at the fair.

____ 4. Many people are looking for jobs.

____ 5. Pablo is a high school student.

____ 6. Paula is looking for a job.

____ 7. Paula is giving information to people at the fair.

____ 8. The fair is noisy because people are talking.

____ 9. Everyone is wearing a suit.

____ 10. Everyone is walking around.

B Fill in the blanks with verbs in the present continuous tense.

	PART 1 *BE*	PART 2 verb + *ing*	
1. It (rain)	is	raining	.
2. Many people (look)			for jobs.
3. The reporter (hold)			a microphone.
4. The reporter (wear)			a suit.
5. Pablo (wear)			blue jeans.
6. The reporter (look)			at Paula.
7. Paula (talk)			to the reporter.
8. Paula (listen)			to the reporter's questions.
9. Many people (talk)			.
10. They (talk)			about jobs.
11. They (walk)			around the gym.
12. A young man (talk)			on a cell phone.

VERBS + PREPOSITIONS TO MEMORIZE

listen to
look at
look for
talk about } *someone/something*

talk to — someone

talk on a phone
walk around

C Find the mistakes. Rewrite the sentences. These things are happening *right now*.

1. Pablo is wear blue jeans. Pablo is wearing blue jeans.
2. People are talk. ....
3. Paula standing. ....
4. The reporter is work. ....
5. It raining. ....
6. They is looking for jobs. ....
7. She wearing a suit. ....
8. He talking on a cell phone. ....
9. People is asking questions. ....
10. A man answering questions. ....

Reminder

"People" is a plural noun.

LESSON 40

Present Continuous Tense—Spelling

1. **Add *ing* to most verbs.**

   read-reading

2. **When a verb ends in C (consonant) + *e*, drop (don't use) the *e*. Add *ing*.**

   dance-dancing **write-writing**

3. **When a verb has *one* syllable and ends in CVC, double the last consonant and add *ing*.**

   put-putting **stop-stopping**

4. **Do NOT double the last consonant before *ing* when a verb:**

   a. **ends in *w, x,* or *y*:** **fix-fixing**
   b. **ends in VVC:** **eat-eating**
   c. **has *two or more* syllables with stress on the *first* syllable:**

   vís-it → vís-it-ing **lís-ten → lís-ten-ing**

C = Consonant (b, c, d, f, g, h, j, k, l, m, n, p, q, r, s, t, v, w, x, y, z)

V = Vowel (a, e, i, o, u)

CVC = Consonant + Vowel + Consonant

A Read this radio report about New Year's Eve in New York City. Underline all the verbs in the present continuous tense (*BE* + verb + *ing*.) Then read along as you listen.

It's 11:30 and I'm reporting from Times Square in New York City. It's very cold. The temperature is about 25 degrees. We're waiting for midnight, and we're having a great time. Everyone is wearing warm winter clothes. Some bands are playing music, and people are dancing. They are trying to stay warm. A lot of people are making noise. Some people are smiling and carrying big Happy New Year signs. And some people are sitting down and drinking hot coffee. Maybe they're tired. Some people are eating ice cream cones. And it's so cold!

B Write the number of the spelling rules for each verb.

	Verbs with *-ing*	Base Forms of Verbs	Rule Number
1.	reporting	report	1
2.	waiting	....	....
3.	having	....	....
4.	wearing	....	....
5.	playing	....	....
6.	dancing	....	....
7.	trying	....	....
8.	making	....	....
9.	smiling	....	....
10.	carrying	....	....
11.	sitting	....	....
12.	drinking	....	....
13.	eating	....	....

C Write the verbs in the *-ing* form.

1. People are (look) looking at the clock.
2. They are (celebrate) .... New Year's Eve.
3. The reporter is (enjoy) .... the evening.
4. People are (listen) .... to the reporter.
5. Many people are (have) .... fun.
6. Some people are (carry) .... signs.
7. A baby is (cry) ....
8. A boy is (sit) ....
9. A cell phone is (ring) ....
10. A woman is (answer) .... her cell phone.
11. She is (walk) .... around.
12. A man is (give) .... information to tourists.
13. A baby is (sleep) ....
14. Two teenagers are (run) ....
15. Two children are (play) ....
16. Their parents are (hug) ....

celebrate

carry

answer

hug

LESSON

41 Present Continuous Tense—Negative Statements

Use the negative form of the present continuous tense to talk about what is not happening right now.

The negative form of the present continuous tense has three parts: *BE*, *not*, and verb + *ing*.

	PART 1 *BE*	PART 2 *not*	PART 3 verb + *ing*	Contracted Forms
I	am	not	working.	I'm not working.
You	are	not	working.	You aren't/You're not working.
He	is	not	working.	He isn't/He's not working.
She	is	not	working.	She isn't/She's not working.
It	is	not	working.	It isn't/It's not working.
We	are	not	working.	We aren't/We're not working.
They	are	not	working.	They aren't/They're not working.

A Look at the two pictures of the Miller family. Read the sentences and check Wednesday night or Friday night. Listen to the tape to check your answers.

Wednesday night

Friday night

		Wednesday night	Friday night
1.	a. Mrs. Miller is reading the newspaper.	✔	
	b. Mrs. Miller isn't reading the newspaper.		✔
2.	a. She isn't playing cards.		
	b. She is playing cards.		
3.	a. David isn't working on the computer.		
	b. David is working on the computer.		
4.	a. Jon and Pam are doing their homework.		
	b. Jon and Pam aren't doing their homework.		
5.	a. Jon and Pam aren't watching TV.		
	b. Jon and Pam are watching TV.		

B Write what you and your classmates are NOT doing right now. Use these verbs. Read your sentences to your partner.

cook	sleep	watch TV	drive	play cards
send e-mail	listen to music	take a walk	do laundry	have dinner

(You) I'm at school.

1. I'm not cooking.
2. ....

(Your partner) You're at school.

3. You
4. ....

(Your teacher) She's/He's at school.

5. She/He
6. ....

(You and your partner) We're at school.

7. We
8. ....

(Your classmates) They're at school.

9. They
10. ....

C Write negative sentences with *It*. Use the present continuous tense.

1. The dog is sleeping. (eat) It isn't eating.
2. The bird is sitting. (fly) ....
3. The phone is quiet. (ring) ....
4. The weather is nice. (rain) ....
5. The computer is broken. (work) ....

D Chant

She's reading a magazine.

She's reading a magazine.
She's not reading a book.
She's studying computers.
She's not learning to cook.

He's practicing English.
He's not practicing Greek.
He's not learning to write,
But he's learning how to speak.

He's staying in Miami
With his rich uncle Ray.
He's not staying long,
But he's not leaving today.

LESSON

42 Present Continuous Tense—Yes-No Questions and Short Answers

Ask Yes-No questions in the present continuous tense to ask if something is happening right now.

To make a Yes-No question with the present continuous tense, put the *BE* part of the verb first.

Statement: **I am dancing.**

Yes-No Question: **Am I dancing?**

Questions	**Short Answers**		
	Affirmative (No Contraction)	**Negative**	
Am I dancing?	Yes, you are.	No, you aren't.	No, you're not.
Are you going home?	Yes, I am. Yes, we are.	--- No, we aren't.	No, I'm not. No, we're not.
Is he sleeping?	Yes, he is.	No, he isn't.	No, he's not.
Is she driving?	Yes, she is.	No, she isn't.	No, she's not.
Is it raining?	Yes, it is.	No, it isn't.	No, it's not.
Are we making noise?	Yes, we are. Yes, you are.	No, we aren't. No, you aren't.	No, we're not. No, you're not.
Are they wearing jeans?	Yes, they are.	No, they aren't.	No, they're not.

A Look at the pictures. Listen to the questions and circle the answers.

Jerry in Seattle

1. 

Yes, he is. (circled) No, he isn't.

Sue in Chicago

2. 

Yes, she is. No, she isn't.

Nick and Alex in Miami

3. 

Yes, they are. No, they aren't.

London

4. 

Yes, it is. No, it isn't.

B Write Yes-No questions about the pictures in Exercise A. Use the present continuous tense. Then answer the questions with short answers.

1. Jerry/wake up ..... Is Jerry waking up ..... ? ..... Yes, he is. .....
2. Jerry/smile .... ? ....
3. Sue/sit down .... ? ....
4. Sue/stand .... ? ....
5. Nick and Alex/ride bikes .... ? ....
6. Nick and Alex/swim .... ? ....
7. It/rain .... in London? ....
8. It/snow .... in London? ....

C Write Yes-No questions and short answers. Use the present continuous tense.

1.

(I/wear)

Am I wearing the right clothes?

No, you're not.

2.

(I/make)

.... too much noise?

....

3.

(we/go)

.... too fast?

....

4.

(you/study)

.... English right now?

....

D On a small piece of paper, write a sentence in the present continuous tense with "I." Your teacher will collect the sentences. Students will take turns acting out the sentences and the class will guess what they are doing.

EXAMPLE sentence: I'm driving.

EXAMPLE question: Are you playing the piano?

EXAMPLE answers: No, I'm not./Yes, I am.

LESSON 43

Present Continuous Tense—Wh Questions and Short Answers

Ask Wh Questions in the present continuous tense to get information about what is happening *right now*.

***What, Where,* and *Why* Questions**	**Short Answers**
What are you watching? Where are you going? Why are you crying?	A video. To the movies. Because I'm sad.
Who* Questions—Use *Who is* when you want to know *who is doing something.	
Who is (Who's) babysitting? Who is (Who's) watching TV?	Kelly is. The twins are.
Special Questions	
How is (How's) it going? How are you doing? What are you doing?	Fine. Fine. And you? Reading.
Use *When* with the present continuous tense to ask about the future.	
When are you coming home?	After the movie.

A Emily and Rick are out for the evening. The babysitter is talking to Emily. Listen to the conversation. Then match the questions and answers.

d 1. How's it going?
...... 2. What's the baby doing?
...... 3. What are the boys doing?
...... 4. Why is Janie crying?
...... 5. Where are the parents going?
...... 6. When are the parents coming home?

a. Watching TV.
b. Because she wants her Mommy.
c. To the movies.
~~d.~~ Fine.
e. After the movie.
f. Sleeping.

B It is one hour later. What's happening? Put the words in the correct order to make Wh questions.

1. doing/babysitter/is/the/What .... What is the babysitter doing?
2. doing/baby/is/the/What ....
3. What/Janie/doing/is ....
4. wearing/Janie/What/is ....
5. twins/are/What/the/doing ....
6. the/twins/are/wearing/What ....

C Look at the picture. Write answers to the questions in Exercise B.

1. a. (hold) .... She's holding the baby.
   b. (give) .... the baby a bottle.
   c. (sit) .... in a rocking chair.
2. (drink) ....
3. (sleep) ....
4. (wear) .... pajamas.
5. (watch) .... TV.
6. (wear) .... pajamas.

D Write questions for the answers. Look at the picture in Exercise A.

1. (Who) .... is crying? Janie is.
2. (Why) ....? Because she wants her mommy.
3. (Who) ....? The twins are.
4. (Where) ....? To the movies.
5. (Why) ....? Because they want to have a nice evening together.
6. (When) ....? After the movie.
7. (How) ....? The children are fine.

Lessons 39–43

Review

The Present Continuous Tense

A Dictation Two friends are talking on the phone. Listen to the conversation and write what you hear. Key words: *chicken, rice*.

A: What are ....?

B: ....

A: ....?

B: ....

B Write the *–ing* form of the verb.

See inside back cover for spelling rules.

1. eat	eating	**7.** run	....
2. take	....	**8.** stay	....
3. use	....	**9.** sit	....
4. study	....	**10.** drive	....
5. play	....	**11.** come	....
6. have	....	**12.** stop	....

C Complete the sentences with the words below. Use the present continuous tense. Use contractions with subject pronouns.

work	sleep	rain	wear	drink
watch	read	laugh	sit	cry

Reminder

The present continuous tense has two parts.

1. Mrs. Miller is reading the newspaper.
2. She .... on the couch.
3. She .... a cup of tea.
4. The children .... TV.
5. They .... because it's a funny program.
6. They .... pajamas.
7. Mr. Miller .... on the computer.
8. Listen! The baby ....
9. The weather is bad. It .... outside.
10. The cat .... on the couch.

D Write *true* sentences. Use affirmative or negative statements.

EXAMPLE: It (snow) isn't snowing now.

1. It (rain) .... now.
2. We (do) .... an exercise in the grammar book.
3. We (take) .... a test right now.
4. The teacher (write) .... on the blackboard right now.
5. The teacher (wear) .... a sweater.
6. The teacher (sit) .... down right now. The teacher (stand) .... up.
7. The students in this room (sit) .... in a circle.
8. I (wear) .... a watch right now.
9. I (wear) .... jeans.
10. Many students in this class (wear) .... jeans.

E Read the telephone conversation between a mother and her daughter. Complete the sentences.

Mother: Hi! How (1. you/do) .... ?

Daughter: (2. we/do) .... fine. How about you?

Mother: I'm fine. What (3. the children/do) .... ?

Daughter: (4. Susan/check) .... her e-mail and (5. the boys/play) .... a game.

Mother: (6. the baby/sleep) .... ?

Daughter: No. (7. I/hold) .... him now because (8. he/cry) ....

Mother: I hear him now....Oh, how's the weather? (9. it/rain) .... ?

Daughter: Yes, it is. (10. it/rain) .... very hard.

LESSONS 39–43 Have Fun

A Crossword Puzzle

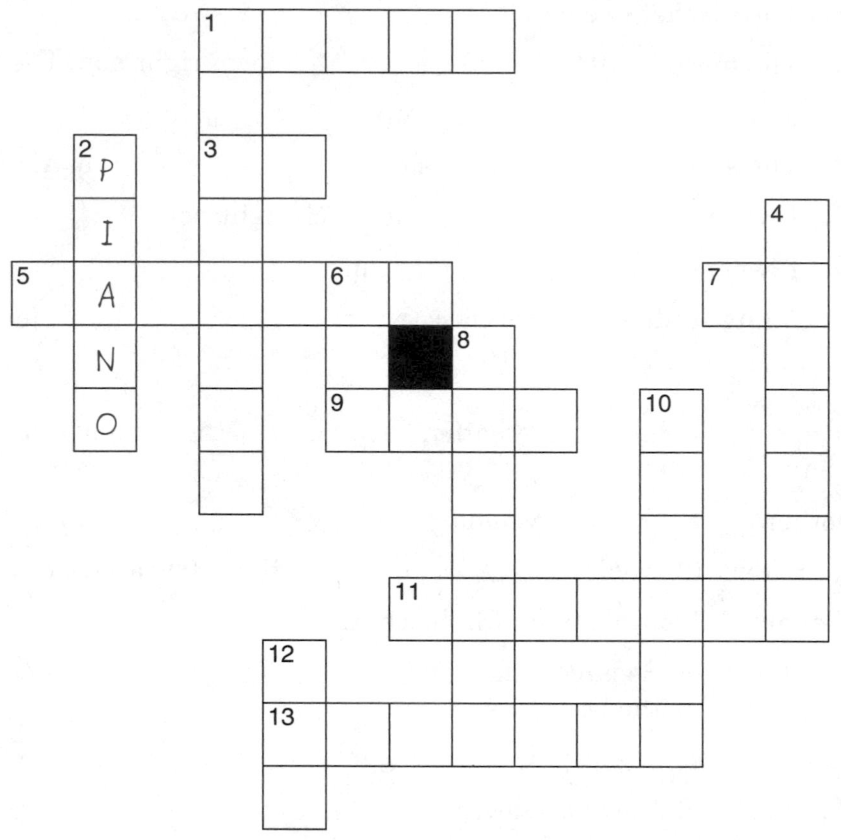

Across

1. I'm .... my homework.
3. She .... helping her mother.
5. He's .... on the phone.
7. Are you going home? Yes, I ....
9. Are the children studying? No, ... 're not.
11. I usually sit in the front row. Today I'm .... in the back row.
13. Listen! The telephone is .... !

Down

1. She's .... a glass of water.
2. Listen! She's playing the ....
4. The baby is .... because she is happy.
6. Is she watching TV? No, she's ....
8. I'm .... jeans today.
10. He's not laughing. He's .... !
12. We .... working hard in this class.

B Chant

What are you doing?

What are you doing?
I'm talking to Rose.
What's she doing?
She's packing her clothes.

Where is she going?
She's going to Spain.
How is she going?
She's taking a plane.

Who's going with her?
Her husband Bob.
Why are they going?
Because she got a job.

LESSON 44

Contrast: Present and Present Continuous Tenses

Use the present tense to talk about something that repeats or is routine.

		He	**studies**	**every day.**
	Does	**she**	**study**	**on Mondays?**
Where	**do**	**they**	**study?**	

Use the present continuous tense to talk about what is happening right now.

		I	**am studying**	**right now.**
	Are	**you**	**studying**	**today?**
Where	**is**	**he**	**studying?**	

TIME EXPRESSIONS

Present	**Present Continuous**
every second/minute/hour/day/ week/weekend/month/year	**now**
once a day, twice a week, three times a month, on Tuesdays	**right now**

A Read this story about two retired people, Maggie and James. Underline the verbs. Then listen to the story as you read along.

Routine

Every day Maggie gets up early. She gets dressed, and she goes to the park. She walks for an hour with a friend. Then she goes back home and takes a shower. She eats breakfast, and then she puts on her uniform. She works in a hospital three times a week.

Routine

James wakes up every day around 8:00. He exercises, and then he takes a shower. He eats toast and fruit for breakfast. Then he reads the newspaper. Around 11:00, he drives to a homeless shelter. He works there every weekday for two hours. He serves lunch.

Right Now

Right now, Maggie and James are getting married. Maggie is wearing a beautiful dress. She is holding flowers. James is wearing a nice suit. They are standing together and holding hands. They are smiling.

B Look at the verbs in Exercise A. Which verbs show what Maggie and James do as routine? Which verbs show what they're doing right now? Write the verbs on the lines.

Routine		Right Now
gets up		are getting married

C On the left, write *N* if the action in the sentence is happening NOW. Write *R* if the action REPEATS or is ROUTINE. Then fill in the blanks with the verbs in parentheses. Use the present tense or present continuous tense.

R **1.** Maggie (get dressed) gets dressed early every morning.

N **2.** She (get dressed) is getting dressed right now.

____ **3.** She (put on) ____________ her uniform after breakfast.

____ **4.** She (negative--wear) ____________ her uniform every day.

____ **5.** She (negative--wear) ____________ her uniform right now.

____ **6.** Right now, Maggie (get) ____________ married to James.

____ **7.** They (smile) ____________ because they are happy today.

____ **8.** (smile) ____________ they ____________ right now?

____ **9.** (work) ____________ James ____________ right now?

get dressed

put on

D Chant

Once a week he calls his mother.

Once a week, he calls his mother.
Twice a week, he calls his brother.
Every day he calls his friends.
Right now, he's talking on the phone.

Every day, he does the dishes.
Every day, he does the dishes.
Once a week, he does the laundry.
Right now, he's talking on the phone.

Once a week, he cooks spaghetti.
Once a week, he cooks spaghetti.
Twice a week, he orders pizza.
Right now, he's talking on the phone.

LESSON 45

Contrast: *BE* and *DO* in Present Tense Negative Statements and Questions

Use a form of *BE* with a noun, an adjective, or a place, to make a negative statement or a question in the present tense.

Use a form of *BE* to make a negative statement or a question in the present continuous tense.

	Negative Statements	**Questions**
with nouns:	He isn't a doctor. You aren't a nurse.	Is he a doctor? Are you a nurse?
with adjectives:	I'm not late. It isn't expensive.	Am I late? Is it expensive?
with places:	She isn't at work. They aren't there.	Is she at work? Are they there?
with the present continuous tense:	He isn't working. We aren't going to the party.	Is he working? Are we going to the party?

Use a form of *DO* with all other verbs to make a negative sentence or a question in the present tense. *DO* is a helping verb.

	Negative Statements	**Questions**
with all verbs:	I **don't work** on Monday. You **don't live** here. He **doesn't study** English. It **doesn't work**. We **don't have** the book. They **don't want** pizza.	**Do** I **work** on Monday? **Do** you **live** here? **Does** he **study** English? **Does** it **work**? **Do** we **have** the book? **Do** they **want** pizza?
Correct: **Incorrect:**	**Do** you live here? ~~Are you live here?~~	She **isn't** single. ~~She doesn't single.~~

See Lesson 5 to review nouns, adjectives, and verbs.

A Maggie is answering questions. First, read the questions and circle the correct answers. Then listen to check your answers.

1.	Do you work, Maggie?	Yes, I am.	(Yes, I do.)
2.	Do you wear a uniform?	Yes, I am.	Yes, I do.
3.	Are you single?	No, I'm not.	No, I don't.
4.	Do you have children?	Yes, I am.	Yes, I do.
5.	Does your daughter have children?	Yes, she is.	Yes, she does.
6.	Do your grandchildren visit you a lot?	Yes, they are.	Yes, they do.
7.	Are they noisy?	Yes, they are.	Yes, they do.
8.	Are they visiting you right now?	Yes, they are.	Yes, they do.

B First, read the questions. Then on the left, write one of the following:

BE—adjective *BE*—noun *BE*—place

BE—PCT (present continuous tense) *DO*—verb

Then, answer the questions. Write *true* short answers.

BE-noun	**1.** Are you a student?	Yes, I am.
....	**2.** Are you at school?	....
....	**3.** Are you studying English?	....
....	**4.** Does your teacher give homework?	....
....	**5.** Do you do your homework?	....
....	**6.** Are your classmates working hard right now?	....
....	**7.** Do they work hard every day?	....
....	**8.** Is your English class in the U.S.?	....
....	**9.** Are you from Canada?	....
....	**10.** Do you come from Europe?	....
....	**11.** Are you Asian?	....
....	**12.** Is it raining?	....
....	**13.** Do you like ice cream?	....

C Underline the main verbs in the *DO*—verb questions in Exercise B.

EXAMPLE: **4.** Does your teacher give homework?

D Write eight true negative statements. Write four sentences with *BE* and four sentences with *DO*. Share your sentences with a partner.

EXAMPLE: I'm not hungry.

BE (am not/isn't/aren't)

1. I ....

2. My teacher ....

3. My classmates ....

4. We ....

DO (don't/doesn't)

5. I ....

6. My teacher ....

7. My classmates ....

8. We ....

LESSON 46

CAN—Affirmative and Negative Statements

And *and* But

Can is a helping verb. It shows ability. *Can't* = *cannot*.

	Helping Verb	Base Form of Main Verb	
I You He She It We They	can can't	speak speak	English. English.

Correct:	I can speak English.
Incorrect:	I can ~~to~~ speak English. He can speak~~s~~ English.

Statements with *and* and *but*

They can speak English,	**and**	they can speak Chinese.
They can speak English,	**but**	they can't speak Japanese.

Pronunciation:	I can spéak English (say *can* fast)	I cán't spéak English. (say *can't* strongly)

A Listen to the news report about a family of Martians. The report is about what the family *can* do, and what it *can't* do. As you listen, circle *can* or *can't*.

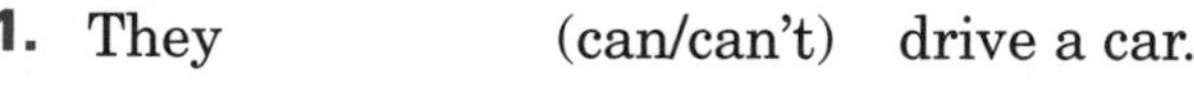

1. They (can/can't) drive a car.
2. They (can/can't) fly.
   and they (can/can't) walk.
3. They (can/can't) swim.
4. The children (can/can't) play tennis,
   but they (can/can't) play basketball.
5. The girl (can/can't) play the violin.
6. They (can/can't) use computers.
7. They (can/can't) speak many languages,
   but they (can/can't) read or write.
8. Their dog (can/can't) read.
9. It also (can/can't) write.
10. They (can/can't) fix their spaceship.

B Read what Martian and Earth children say. Then complete the chart.

Hi. I'm Marty from Mars. I can fly, but I can't swim.

And I'm Eddie. I'm from Earth. I can't fly, but I can fly a kite.

My name is Margie. I come from Mars. I can play the violin and guitar, but I can't play the piano.

I'm Annie. I'm not from Mars. I'm from Earth. I can't understand the Martian language, but I can speak English, Chinese, and Spanish.

	Can	Can't
1. Marty from Mars	fly	
2. Eddie from Earth		
3. Margie from Mars		
4. Annie from Earth		

C Find the mistakes. Rewrite the sentences.

1. I can to speak English. I can speak English.
2. She can speaks four languages. ......
3. We can't speak English, and we can speak Vietnamese. ......
4. We can speak English, but we can speak Vietnamese. ......
5. You can to speak English very well. ......

D Use some of the verbs in this lesson, and write three sentences about what you *can* do and three sentences about what you *can't* do. Then write one sentence with *and* and one sentence with *but*. Read your sentences to a partner.

EXAMPLE: CAN: I can play soccer. I can play the guitar. I can speak English.
CAN'T: I can't swim. I can't fly. I can't play tennis.

AND: I can't swim and I can't fly.
BUT: I can play soccer, but I can't play tennis.

LESSON 47

CAN—Yes-No Questions and Short Answers

Use can to ask questions about ability.

Statement:	**He**	**can**	**play the piano.**
Question:	**Can**	**he**	**play the piano?**

Question			**Short Answer**		
	I			**I**	
	you			**you**	
	he		**Yes,**	**he**	**can.**
Can	**she**	**play?**		**she**	
	it		**No,**	**it**	**can't.**
	we			**we**	
	they			**they**	

A Look at the pictures. Listen to the questions and circle the answers.

Harry

Gabriela and Howie

1.	Yes, he can.	No, he can't.	**5.**	Yes, they can.	No, they can't.
2.	Yes, he can.	No, he can't.	**6.**	Yes, they can.	No, they can't.
3.	Yes, he can.	No, he can't.	**7.**	Yes, they can.	No, they can't.
4.	Yes, he can.	No, he can't.	**8.**	Yes, they can.	No, they can't.

B Gabriela wants to work at a summer camp as a counselor. Read the information about her. Write questions and answers on her application.

Gabriela is a 16-year-old high school student. She likes sports. She can play tennis, basketball, volleyball, baseball, and soccer. She can play the piano and drums. She can't sing. She can't draw. She baby-sits a lot. She knows a lot about nature—trees, flowers, birds, and insects.

COUNSELOR APPLICATION

Please answer the following questions.

1. Can you play sports? Yes, I can. I can play tennis, basketball, volleyball, baseball and soccer.
2. .... play musical instruments? ....
3. .... sing? ....
4. .... draw? ....
5. .... work with young children? ....
6. .... teach children about nature? ....

C Ask your classmates these questions. When a classmate answers "Yes," write his or her first name under the question. Do this in five minutes. The student with the most names wins.

1. Can you understand some English on TV?
2. Can you use a computer?
3. Can you ride a bike?
4. Can you play tennis?
5. Can you swim?
6. Can you cook good food?
7. Can you play a musical instrument?

Lessons 44–47

Review

Present Tense vs. Present Continuous Tense, *BE* vs. *DO*, *CAN*

A Dictation Listen to the paragraph about a student in her classroom. Write what you hear. Key words: *sweater, winter*.

Right now ....

....

....

B Write a paragraph about what you are doing now. Use the paragraph in Exercise A as a model.

Right now ....

....

....

C Complete the questions with *Is, Are, Does,* or *Do*. Then, answer the questions with *true* short answers.

		Questions	Short Answers
1.	Do	you play soccer?	Yes, I do.
2.	Are	you playing soccer now?	No, I'm not.
3.	....	you work hard every day?	....
4.	....	you working hard now?	....
5.	....	your teacher give homework?	....
6.	....	your teacher wear glasses?	....
7.	....	your teacher wearing glasses right now?	....
8.	....	your teacher here today?	....
9.	....	you live in the U.S.?	....
10.	....	you a new student at this school?	....
11.	....	you tired right now?	....
12.	....	you doing this exercise?	....
13.	....	you want to finish this exercise?	....
14.	....	it cold today?	....
15.	....	it rain a lot?	....

D Compare the present tense and the present continuous tense. Complete the chart.

	Present Tense		Present Continuous Tense	
	Affirmative	**Negative**	**Affirmative**	**Negative**
1. He (study)	He studies.	He doesn't study.	He's studying.	He isn't studying.
2. I (work)		I don't work.		
3. You (smoke)				
4. She (cry)				
5. He (watch)	TV.	TV.	TV.	He isn't watching TV.
6. We (run)				

E Complete the chart. Use *can*.

	Affirmative	Negative	Question
1.			Can they speak English?
2.		He can't play guitar.	
3.	She can play tennis.		
4.		They can't dance.	
5.			Can we go home?

LESSONS 44–47

Have Fun

A Crossword Puzzle

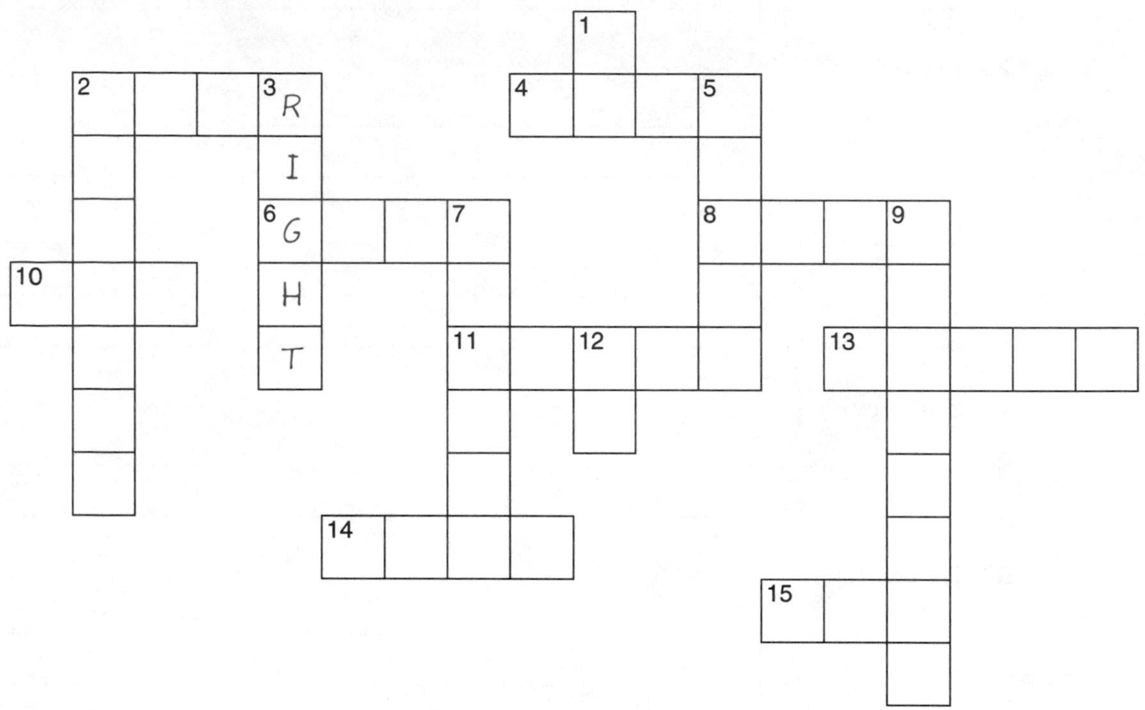

Across

2. Do you .... glasses?
4. Do you .... from Mexico?
6. My mother .... shopping once a week.
8. He .... cereal for breakfast every day.
10. .... you busy today?
11. Are the children quiet or .... ?
13. He usually .... the newspaper.
14. .... this classroom have a TV?
15. I .... play tennis, but I can't play basketball.

Down

1. .... you like this puzzle?
2. Are you .... glasses now?
3. I'm not home .... now. I'm in school.
5. I work .... day.
7. Are you married or .... ?
9. Shh! The baby is ....
12. .... this puzzle difficult?

B Chant

Things They Can and Can't Do

She can swim very well,
But she can't dive.
He can ride a bike,
But he can't drive.
He can cook spaghetti,
But he can't cook well.
They can speak Chinese,
But they can't write or spell.
I can play the piano,
But I can't sing.
Early in the morning
I can't do a thing.

LESSON 48

Past Tense of BE—Affirmative and Negative Statements

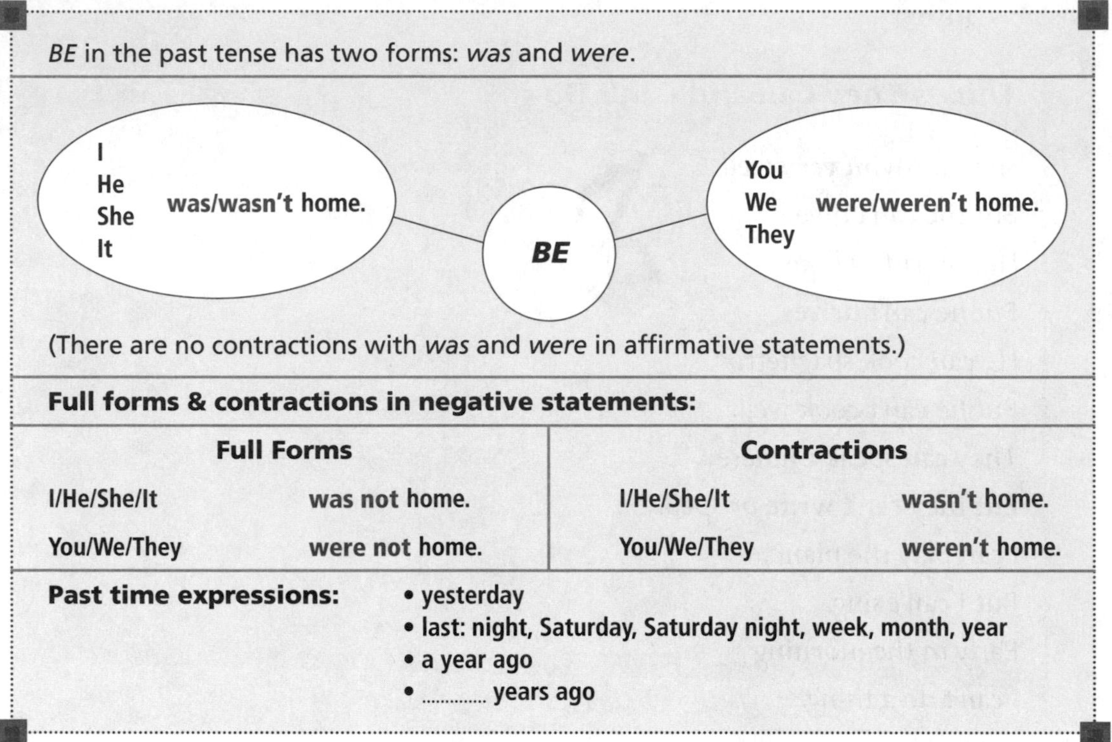

BE in the past tense has two forms: *was* and *were*.

(There are no contractions with *was* and *were* in affirmative statements.)

Full forms & contractions in negative statements:

Full Forms		Contractions	
I/He/She/It	was not home.	I/He/She/It	wasn't home.
You/We/They	were not home.	You/We/They	weren't home.

Past time expressions:
- yesterday
- last: night, Saturday, Saturday night, week, month, year
- a year ago
- .... years ago

A Look at the pictures. Listen to the telephone conversations. Write the number of the conversation that goes with each picture.

were = past tense form of BE

"*we're*" = "*we are*"

A.

....

B.

....

C.

...1...

D.

....

B Change these sentences from the present to the past tense.

	Now	*Last Saturday night...*
1.	Norma and Rick are at a restaurant.	Norma and Rick were at a restaurant.
2.	It is their anniversary.	
3.	It isn't Norma's birthday.	
4.	Norma is beautiful in her white dress.	
5.	Rick is handsome in his new suit.	
6.	They are at a window table.	
7.	They aren't near the kitchen.	
8.	There are flowers on the table.	
9.	The food is delicious.	
10.	It isn't cheap, but it isn't very expensive.	
11.	The waiter is very friendly.	
12.	There is nice music.	
13.	There aren't many people there.	
14.	It is a very special evening.	

C **Guessing Game** Write six *true* sentences and three *false* sentences about the past.

EXAMPLE: Last summer: I was in Hawaii. I was busy. I was a student.

When?	*I was* + place	*I was* + Adjective	*I was* + Noun
Last summer:			
Last year:			
Ten years ago:			

Now read your sentences to your partner. Your partner will guess the sentences that are false. Your partner can say: *You weren't in Hawaii last summer. You were home.*

LESSON 49

Past Tense of *BE* —Yes-No Questions and Short Answers

Questions with Or

Statement:	You	were	famous.
Yes-No Question:	Were	you	famous?

Yes/No Questions	Short Answers	
Was I rich?	Yes, you were.	No, you weren't.
Were you married?	Yes, I was.	No, I wasn't.
Was he divorced?	Yes, he was.	No, he wasn't.
Was she a musician?	Yes, she was.	No, she wasn't.
Was it good?	Yes, it was.	No, it wasn't.
Were we musicians?	Yes, we were.	No, we weren't.
	Yes, you were.	No, you weren't.
Were they in Los Angeles?	Yes, they were.	No, they weren't.
OR: Were you married or single?	Married./I was married.	

A Thirty years ago, Zach was a famous rock star. Now he's 70 years old. Listen to this radio interview and circle the answers to the questions.

1.	Was Zach very famous?	(Yes, he was.)	No, he wasn't.
2.	Was he a good musician?	Yes, he was.	No, he wasn't.
3.	Was he rich?	Yes, he was.	No, he wasn't.
4.	Was he married or single?	Married.	Single.
5.	Was his wife a guitarist?	Yes, she was.	No, she wasn't.
6.	Was she a drummer?	Yes, she was.	No, she wasn't.
7.	Were they in San Francisco or Los Angeles?	In San Francisco.	In Los Angeles.
8.	Were they on TV?	Yes, they were.	No, they weren't.
9.	Was Zach on the radio?	Yes, he was.	No, he wasn't.

B Write Yes-No questions and answers about Zach, his wife, Patty, their children, and their house.

Thirty years ago...

1.

Question: Was she happy?

Answer: Yes, she was.

2.

Question: .... big?

Answer: ....

3.

Question: .... divorced?

Answer: ....

4.

Question: .... in an office?

Answer: ....

5.

Question: .... poor?

Answer: ....

6.

Question: .... a doctor?

Answer: ....

C Look at the pictures in Exercise B. Answer these questions.

Thirty years ago...

1. Was Patty happy or sad? She was happy.
2. Was she married or divorced? ....
3. Were Patty and Zach rich or poor? ....
4. Was their house big or small? ....
5. Were they in an office or at their pool? ....
6. Was Zach a doctor or a musician? ....

LESSON

50 Past Tense of *BE*—Wh Questions and Short Answers

Questions and Answers with was/were born

Statement:	You were on vacation.
WH-Question:	When were you on vacation? In January.

Questions	**Short Answers**
Where were you on vacation?	In Brazil.
When were you on vacation?	In January.
Why were you on vacation in January?	Because it's summer there in January.
How long were you on vacation?	For two weeks.
How was your vacation?	Great!
***Who* Question**	
Who was on vacation?	I was./We were./Joanne was./Joanne.
See Lesson 24 for present tense *Who* questions with *BE*.	
Expression: *BE* (was-were) born	
Where were you born?	In Seoul, Korea./I was born in Seoul, Korea.
When was he born?	In 1970./He was born in 1970.

Correct:	I **was born** in the U.S.	They **were born** in 1972.
Incorrect:	~~I born in the U.S.~~	~~They born in 1972.~~

A Read the questions. Listen to the conversation. Then read the questions again and circle the answers.

1.	Who was on vacation?	(Laura.)	Lin.
2.	Where was she?	In Mexico.	In Taiwan.
3.	When was her vacation?	Last week.	Last month.
4.	How was her vacation?	Terrible.	Wonderful.
5.	How long was her vacation?	Two months.	Two weeks.
6.	Who was with her?	Her sisters.	Her children.
7.	Were Laura and Lin born in the U.S.?	Yes, they were.	No, they weren't.
8.	Who was born in Mexico?	Laura was.	Laura's children were.
9.	Who was born in Taiwan?	Lin was.	Lin's children were.
10.	Was Lin on vacation last week?	Yes, she was.	No, she wasn't.

Pronunciation: "Where" and "wear" sound like "air." "Were" sounds like "her."

B Put the words in the correct order to make Yes-No and Wh questions with *was* and *were*. Then write short answers.

	Questions	Short Answers
1.	born/you/the U.S./Were/in Were you born in the U.S.?	No, I wasn't.
2.	Where/born/you/were	....
3.	you/When/born/were	....
4.	weekend/last/were/you/Where	....
5.	was/weekend/How/your	....
6.	yesterday/school/Were/at/you	....
7.	at/Why/school/you/were	....
8.	long/Monday/How/school/at/you/were/last	....

C Ask two classmates the questions from Exercise B. Write their answers in the chart.

	SHORT ANSWERS	
	Classmate 1:	**Classmate 2:** ....
1		
2		
3		
4		
5		
6		
7		
8		

Now write eight sentences about one of your classmates.

EXAMPLE: *Lisa wasn't born in the U.S.*

LESSON

51 Contrast: Past and Present Tenses of *BE*

Use the verb *BE* with adjectives, nouns, and places.

	Present Tense: *am/is/are*	**Past Tense: *was/were***
with adjectives:	**Now I'm married.**	**A year ago, I was single.**
with nouns:	**She's a lawyer.**	**She was a student.**
with places:	**They're at home tonight.**	**They were at a party last night.**

More past time expressions: a long time ago, in 1990, when I was 10 years old

A Read about Ken and Sally. Listen to the tape and fill in the blanks with present and past forms of *BE*. Use contractions when it's possible. Then practice reading about these people with a partner.

both = two

In 1990, I ___was___ in Korea. I ________ single and I ________ a student. My friends ________ students, too. We ________ together all the time. Now I ________ in the United States. I ________ not single. I ________ married. My wife and I ________ always together. We ________ both lawyers and we ________ very busy. But we ________ with our friends on weekends.

A long time ago, my husband and I ________ rich. We ________ famous movie stars in Hollywood. Now life ________ different. We ________ not married and we ________ not rich. And we ________ not famous! I ________ in Toronto, and my ex-husband ________ in Dallas. I ________ a restaurant owner, and he ________ a teacher. I ________ happy, and he ________ too!

B Talk about Jerry and Elaine. Fill in the blanks with *am, is, are, was,* or *were*.

1. Ten years ago, Jerry __was__ in fifth grade. Today he ______ in college.
2. Ten years ago, Elaine ______ eight years old. Now, she ______ 18.
3. When Jerry ______ 10, he ______ short. He ______ tall now.
4. When Elaine ______ 8, she ______ short. Today she ______ still short.
5. Jerry and Elaine ______ lazy when they ______ children. Now, they (negative) ______ lazy. They work hard.

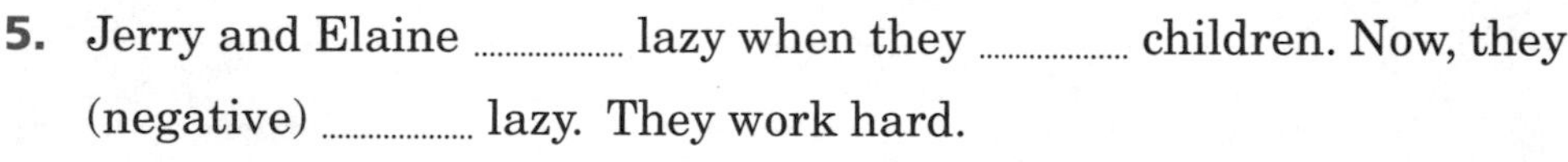

6. Today, Jerry ______ a good student. Ten years ago, he (negative) ______ a good student.

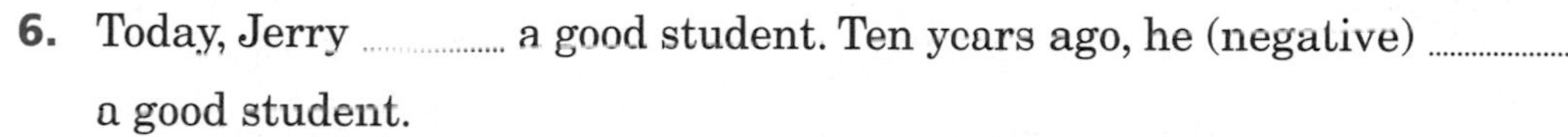

7. Jerry and Elaine (negative) ______ friends when they ______ kids. Now, they ______ boyfriend and girlfriend.

C On a separate piece of paper, rewrite Jerry's sentences in the past tense. Start with "Yesterday." Rewrite Elaine's sentences in the present tense. Start with "Right now."

EXAMPLE: *Jerry: Yesterday I was in the city.*

Jerry: Right now I'm in the city. I'm with my friend Elaine. We're at a nice restaurant. The food is good, but it isn't cheap.

Elaine: Yesterday I was with Jerry. We weren't at school. We were at my house. Jerry and my dad were in the garden. My mother and I were in the kitchen. My sister wasn't home.

D Chant

Sam's a good lawyer.

Sam's a good lawyer.
He's 37.
He was silly
When he was eleven.

Anne's an A student
at Central State.
She was lazy
When she was eight.

John's very serious.
He works hard too.
He wasn't serious
When he was two.

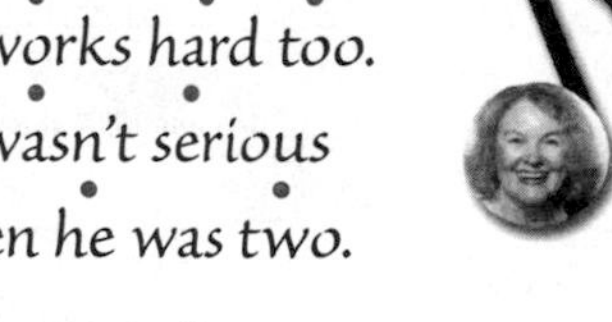

Lisa's very famous.
She's 97.
She was a movie star
When she was eleven.

Lessons 48–51

Review

Past Tense of *BE*
Contrast Past and Present Tenses of *BE*

A Dictation Listen to the paragraph about last Saturday in the city. Write what you hear. Key words: *restaurant, cheap.*

Last ....

....

....

....

B Write *am, is, are, was,* or *were* on the lines.

My life ...is... very different today. Five years ago, I .... in my country. My life .... hard, but my parents .... near me. Now I .... in the U.S., and my parents .... far away. Five years ago, I .... single. I .... a teacher in my country. Now I .... married. My wife .... American. We .... both students. We have a son. Our son .... born last year. Now he .... almost one year old!

C Write a paragraph about yourself. Use the paragraph in Exercise B as a model.

My life is very different today. Five years ago, I ....

....

....

....

....

....

....

....

....

....

D Write questions about a party with *When, Where, How*, and *How Long*. Write a Yes-No question for number 7.

1. A: How was the party?

   B: It was great!

2. A: ______________________________?

   B: It was at a French restaurant.

3. A: ______________________________?

   B: It was last Saturday.

4. A: ______________________________?

   B: It was five hours long.

5. A: ______________________________?

   B: The food was delicious.

6. A: ______________________________?

   B: The music was too loud.

7. A: ______________________________?

   B: Yes, I was very tired.

E Find the mistakes. Rewrite the sentences.

1. I born in Mexico. I was born in Mexico.
2. My children born in the U.S. ______________
3. They don't born in Mexico. ______________
4. Where you were yesterday? ______________
5. How long your vacation? ______________
6. Was difficult the test? ______________
7. My sister she sick last night. ______________
8. The children was late for school. ______________
9. Where the students last night? ______________
10. I don't absent yesterday. ______________
11. I liked the movie. Was interesting. ______________

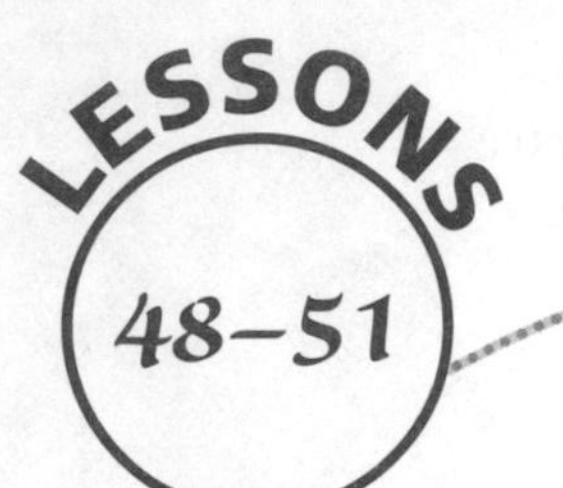

Have Fun

A Walk and Talk Ask three students these questions. Write short notes in the chart.

Questions	Student 1:	Student 2:	Student 3:
1. Where were you five years ago?			
2. Where were you last year?			
3. Where were you last night?			
4. Where were you two hours ago?			

Write sentences about one classmate.

EXAMPLE: *Five years ago, Martin was in his country. Last year, he was in the U.S. Last night, he was at home. Two hours ago, he was at work.*

B Communication Gap Work with a partner. One student will be Student A and the other will be Student B.

Student A: Go to page 199. Follow the directions.
Student B: Go to page 200. Follow the directions.

C Chant

Party Time

We were at the party. Where were you?
We were at the party, too.
I was in the kitchen. Where was Lee?
He was in the living room with me.

Where were all the kids?
They were in the hall.
Where was your old boyfriend, Paul?
Paul wasn't there, neither was Joe.
Where were they?
I don't know.

Where was Jane's new friend Bill?
He was in the dining room with Jill.
The music was fine. The food was great.
The party was over very late.

LESSON

52 Past Tense—Affirmative Statements

Most verbs end in *-ed* to show past tense. These verbs are called "regular verbs."

	Regular Past Tense Verb	Past Time Expressions
I	called my parents	last weekend.
You	walked the dog	last night.
He	watched TV	yesterday.
She	danced	yesterday afternoon.
It	snowed	the day before yesterday.
We	listened to music	on Saturday morning.
They	visited their family	three months ago.

Correct: I needed to work.
Incorrect: I needed to work~~ed~~. (No *ed* on verbs after the word *to*)

Correct: on Saturday morning.
Incorrect: on Saturday ~~in the~~ morning.

Language Notes
Be careful!
- Some words that end in *-ed* are NOT past tense verbs. They are adjectives. They often come after *BE*.

I'm *tired* now. She's *interested* in English.

A Read the postcard from Jose. Underline the past tense verbs. Listen and check your answers. Then practice reading the postcard with a partner.

Greetings from Acapulco. I'm visiting my family in Mexico. I <u>arrived</u> yesterday afternoon. My sister and I walked around our neighborhood on Saturday morning and we talked for two hours. I was interested in all the news. My mom cooked a special dinner, and after dinner we watched family videos.

It was fun. Today I'm tired. I need to rest.

I hope everything is fine in San Francisco!

Take care,

Jose

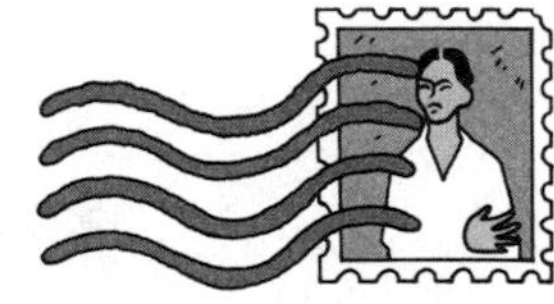

Mr. Chang Lin
4425 Geary Blvd.
San Francisco, CA 94108
USA

B Chang is Jose's friend in San Francisco. Chang is practicing his English. He is writing down everything he did yesterday. Fill in the blanks with the past form of the verbs.

Yesterday, I...

1. (brush) brushed my teeth.
2. (wash) .... my face.
3. (shave) ....
4. (comb) .... my hair.
5. (cook) ....
6. (clean) .... the kitchen.
7. (water) .... the garden.
8. (iron) .... my shirt.
9. (mail) .... my bills.
10. (exercise) .... at the gym.
11. (finish) .... a book.
12. (start) .... a new book.
13. (paint) .... a bookcase.
14. (walk) .... my dog.
15. (call) .... my parents.
16. (visit) .... friends.
17. (rent) .... a DVD.
18. (listen) .... to music.
19. (dance) .... with my friends.
20. (enjoy) .... the evening.

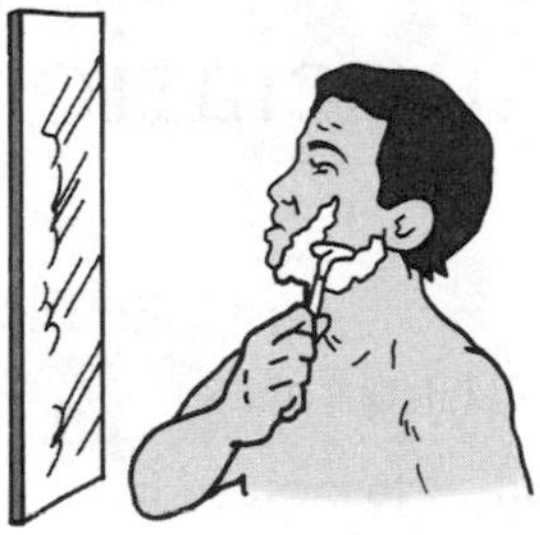

shave

comb

mail

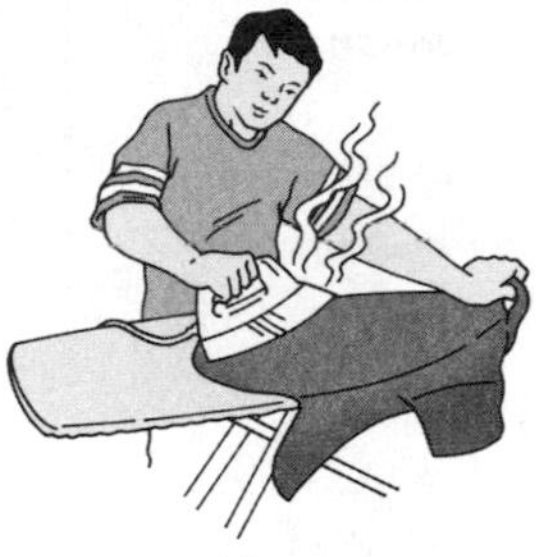

iron

paint

rent

C Change this paragraph from the present tense to the past tense.

Jose is a student at the City College of San Francisco. He wants to be a doctor, and he needs to take many science classes. He likes his classes. In his free time, he plays soccer with his friends. His family is in Mexico, and he sometimes visits them.

Five years ago, Jose ....

....

....

....

....

....

LESSON 53

Past Tense—Spelling and Pronunciation of Regular Verbs

Reminder

C = Consonant
V = Vowel
CVC = Consonant + Vowel + Consonant

ED SPELLING RULES:

1. Add *ed* to most verbs. walk-walked
2. Add *d* to verbs that end in *e*. dance-danced
3. When a verb has *one* syllable and ends in CVC, double the last consonant and add *ed*. stop-stopped

BUT: When a one syllable verb ends in *w*, *x*, or *y*, don't double the last consonant. fax-faxed

4. When a verb ends in a consonant + *y*, drop (don't use) the *y*. Add *ied*. study-studied

BUT: When a verb ends in a vowel + *y*, keep the *y*. play-played

PRONUNCIATION of *ed* endings:

Final Sound of Verb	-ed Pronunciation	New Syllable?	Example
voiceless	/t/	no	walk-walked
voiced	/d/	no	learn-learned
/t/ or/d/	/Id/	yes	want-want•ed need-need•ed

A Read the postcard from Jose. Then listen and practice saying the past tense verbs with *-ed* endings.

Hi again Chang,

I'm having a great time here. It rain**ed** yesterday, so I stay**ed** home and relax**ed**. But when the rain stopp**ed** in the evening, I walk**ed** on the beach with two of my cousins and then we listen**ed** to music at a club. This morning we play**ed** soccer for two hours. Then we visit**ed** friends. But now it's hot and I'm home. I tri**ed** to call you, but you weren't there. So here's a postcard for you.

See you next week!

Jose

Mr. Chang Lin
4425 Geary Blvd.
San Francisco, CA 94108
USA

B Fill in the blanks about Jose's vacation in Mexico. Use the past tense forms of the verbs in the box. Write the number of the spelling rule on the left.

play	dance	smile	hug	carry	end
fix	sip	talk to	stay	visit	show

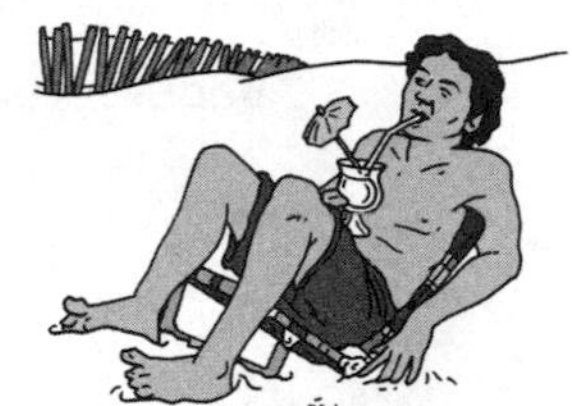

Spelling Rule #

.... **1.** Jose ....danced.... all night at a club.
.... **2.** He .... his friends for three hours.
.... **3.** He .... cold drinks on the beach.
.... **4.** He .... soccer with his cousins.
.... **5.** They .... him in the evening.
.... **6.** His sister .... him pictures of their family.
.... **7.** He .... his mother a lot.
.... **8.** He .... home when the weather was bad.
.... **9.** He .... his father's stereo.
.... **10.** He .... groceries for his mom.
.... **11.** He .... a lot because he was happy.
.... **12.** When his vacation .... , he wasn't happy.

C Write the number of syllables in the verbs in Exercise B.

	Base Form	Number of Syllables	*-ED* Form	Number of Syllables
1.	dance	1	danced	1
2.				
3.				
4.				
5.				
6.				
7.				
8.				
9.				
10.				
11.				
12.				

LESSON

54 Past Tense—Irregular Verbs

Regular verbs end in *ed* to make the past tense.

Base Form	Past Form
want smile	wanted smiled

Irregular verbs don't end in *ed*. Study the past forms of irregular verbs in Appendix D.

Base Form	Past Form
make go	made went

The past form is the same for *I, you, he, she, it, we,* and *they*.

A Read about Annie and Joe. Circle the regular past tense verbs. Underline the irregular past tense verbs. Then listen to the paragraphs. Read the paragraphs aloud with a partner.

Last Saturday morning, Annie went shopping. She bought lettuce, tomatoes, a cucumber, an onion, and carrots. In the evening, at around 6:30, her husband, Joe, made a big salad. He washed and cut the vegetables. Then he put them into a salad bowl. Annie made her special salad dressing with oil and vinegar, and she put it into a jar. She also picked some beautiful flowers from her garden and made a bouquet.

At around 7:00, they got into their car. They took the salad and the bouquet, and they drove to their friend Ken's house for a potluck dinner. They parked near Ken's house. When they got out of their car, they heard music. Annie rang the bell and Ken came to the door. Annie and Joe gave him the bouquet and he smiled and said, "Thank you! Are the flowers from your garden? They're beautiful!" Then he said, "Thanks for the salad. You can put it on the table over there."

Joe put the salad on the table. He put the dressing on the salad. Then he mixed the salad with two long spoons. Annie asked him to dance. They had a great time at the party.

A potluck is a party. Everyone brings food or something to drink.

B There are six regular verbs in Exercise A. Write the base forms and past forms below.

	Base Form	Past Form		Base Form	Past Form
1.	wash	washed	4.		
2.			5.		
3.			6.		

There are 14 different irregular verbs in Exercise A. Write the base forms and past forms below. Write each verb once.

	Base Form	Past Form		Base Form	Past Form
1.	go	went	8.		
2.			9.		
3.			10.		
4.			11.		
5.			12.		
6.			13.		
7.			14.		

C Fill in the blanks with the past tense forms of the irregular verbs in parentheses. Look at Appendix D for the past forms.

1. Annie and Joe (go) ......went...... to the beach last Sunday.
2. They (put) .... beach chairs in their car.
3. They (make) .... a picnic lunch.
4. They (wear) .... bathing suits.
5. They (go) .... swimming.
6. They (sit) .... under a beach umbrella.
7. They (drink) .... water.
8. They (eat) .... lunch around 2 o'clock.
9. Annie (read) .... her book.
10. Joe (take) .... a nap.

LESSON

55 Past Tense—Negative Statements

Did is the past tense of *do*. It is a helping verb. Use *didn't* (*did not*) to make a negative past tense sentence.

Affirmative Statements			**Negative Statements**			
Subject	**Verb**		**Subject**	**Helping Verb**	**Main Verb**	
I	watched	TV.	I	didn't	watch	TV.
You	cleaned	your room.	You	didn't	clean	your room.
He	did	his laundry.	He	didn't	do	his laundry.
She	went	to work.	She	didn't	go	to work.
It	rained.		It	didn't	rain.	
We	studied.		We	didn't	study.	
They	made	dinner.	They	didn't	make	dinner.

To form the negative, use *didn't* + the BASE FORM of the verb.

Correct: I didn't watch TV.
Incorrect: I didn't ~~watched~~ TV.

A Look at the pictures. Then listen to Jeff talk about his week. Under the pictures write *weekend* for Saturday and Sunday. Write *weekday* for Monday, Tuesday, Wednesday, Thursday, or Friday.

A.

weekend

B.

....

C.

....

D.

....

E.

....

F.

....

B The sentences below are NOT true. First, make them negative. Then use Jeff's calendar to write *true* sentences.

JEFF'S WEEK

Sunday	Monday/Tuesday/ Wednesday/Thursday	Friday	Saturday
slept late drank coffee read the paper studied watched TV	got up early went to class ate in the cafeteria went to work did homework	got up early went to class ate in the cafeteria went to work went out to dinner	cleaned made my bed did my laundry went shopping

1. Jeff went to work on Sunday. *Jeff didn't go to work on Sunday.* *He studied and watched TV on Sunday.*
2. Jeff slept late on Tuesday. ....
3. Jeff did his laundry on Monday. ....
4. Jeff went out to dinner on Sunday night. ....
5. Jeff did his homework on Saturday. ....
6. Jeff got up early on Sunday. ....
7. Jeff went to school on Saturday. ....

Now work with a partner to write sentences about what Jeff *didn't do last week*. Look at Jeff's calendar for information.

C Chant

He didn't get up early.

He didn't get up early.
He got up late.
She didn't call at seven.
She called at eight.

He studied English.
He didn't study math.
She took a shower.
She didn't take a bath.

She went to the movies.
She didn't go to bed.
She painted the house blue.
She didn't paint it red.

He made a cup of coffee.
He didn't make tea.
He wrote to his friend.
But he didn't write to me.

LESSON 56

Contrast: *BE* and *DO* in Past Tense Negative Statements

Use a negative past form of *BE*—*wasn't* or *weren't*—with a noun, an adjective or a place to make a negative sentence in the past.

with nouns:	**I/He/She wasn't a student in 1995.** **It wasn't a problem.** **You/We/They weren't students in 1995.**
with adjectives:	**I/He/She wasn't busy yesterday.** **It wasn't cold yesterday.** **You/We/They weren't busy yesterday.**
with places:	**I/He/She wasn't home last weekend.** **It wasn't in the car.** **You/We/They weren't home last weekend.**

Use the negative past form of DO—*didn't* (or *did not*)—with ALL other verbs to make a negative sentence in the past. *Did* is a helping verb.

	Helping Verb	Base Form of Main Verb	
I/You/He/She/ We/They	**didn't**	**go**	**to school last week.**
It	**didn't**	**rain**	**yesterday.**

See Lesson 48 for a review of "wasn't" and "weren't." See Lesson 54 for a review of "didn't."

A Read the paragraphs. Then listen and write *wasn't, weren't,* or *didn't* on the lines.

Tina

Last summer, I __wasn't__ here. I traveled, but I ________ a tourist. I was in my native country. I ________ speak English. I spoke my native language. I ________ go to school and I ________ go to work. I relaxed. I ________ tired. I had a vacation. I was very happy. But I missed my brother, Thomas. We ________ together. He ________ come with me.

Thomas

Last summer, I ________ have a vacation. I ________ go to my native country. I was here. But my sister and my parents ________ here. I stayed here and studied English. In the afternoons and evenings, I worked. I was a taxi driver. I ________ have time to go to the beach. I ________ relax. I was very busy, and I was very tired. But I was happy.

B Look at the negative sentences in Exercise A and complete this chart.

WASN'T/WEREN'T			DIDN'T
With Nouns	**With Adjectives**	**With Places**	**With Verbs**
		here	speak

C Fill in the blanks with *wasn't, weren't,* or *didn't.*

1. Tina ......didn't...... work last summer.
2. She .... get up early.
3. She .... busy or tired.
4. She .... go shopping.
5. She .... in the U.S.
6. Thomas ......wasn't...... in his native country.
7. He .... have free time.
8. He .... take naps.
9. He .... relaxed.
10. Tina and Thomas .... together.
11. They .... take a trip together.
12. They .... see each other.

to travel = to take a trip

D Rewrite this paragraph in the past tense. Then work with a partner. Take turns reading each sentence aloud.

Every summer, Tina visits her family in China. She doesn't go to school and she doesn't work. She doesn't want to be far from her family for a long time. She is relaxed in China, but she isn't relaxed in the U.S. Thomas doesn't go back to China. He doesn't have time. He doesn't want to stop his classes in the summer.

Last summer, Tina visited ....

....

....

....

....

Now write a paragraph about what *you* did on your vacation or last summer. Use the paragraphs in Exercise A as examples.

Lessons 52–56

Review

Past Tense

BE vs. Do

A Dictation Listen to the paragraph about a person from Brazil. Write what you hear. Key words: *Brazil, expensive.*

I was ....

....

....

....

....

B Write a paragraph about yourself. Use the paragraph in Exercise A as a model.

I was ....

....

....

....

....

....

C Complete the chart.

Present		Past	
EVERY DAY		YESTERDAY	
Affirmative	**Negative**	**Affirmative**	**Negative**
I'm tired.	I'm not tired.	I was tired.	....
I work hard.	....	....	I didn't work hard.
He plays soccer.	....	....	....
You are busy.	....	....	....
They study hard.	....	....	....

D Write the *-ed* form of these regular verbs. Check (✔) verbs that have an added syllable.

dance	shop	love	smile
start	cry	try	stop
carry	need	walk	study
sip	hug	like	want

Rule 1 -ed	Rule 2 -d	Rule 3 double consonant +ed	Rule 4 -ied
started ✔			

E Find the mistakes. Rewrite the sentences.

1. I didn't studied last night. I didn't study last night.
2. I staied home yesterday.
3. The girl did liked her present.
4. He wash the dishes last night.
5. I'm worked in Texas last year.
6. You wasn't worked last night.
7. He play tennis two days ago.
8. I needed to worked.
9. They happy last year.
10. I tired last night.
11. She taked two classes last year.
12. We didn't played baseball yesterday afternoon.
13. We eat dinner at 8:00 last night.
14. We wasn't busy yesterday.
15. The baby sleep ten hours yesterday.

Have Fun

A Word Search Write the past tense forms of the verbs in the chart. Then circle the past tense verbs in the puzzle. The words can be vertical (|), horizontal (—), or diagonal (⁄). The words can also be spelled backwards.

Base Form	Past Form	Base Form	Past Form	Base Form	Past Form
carry	carried	go		smile	
drink		make		stop	
eat		play		study	
get		put		take	
give		read		wear	

```
D T E K T F B D T G
D E P P O T S E N O
D D I N U D B I E T
F R T D E T T R W S
E T A L U O R R F D
M D I N O T A A R U
S M A K K T S C E B
S C P M A T E V A B
P L A Y E D A U D J
E R O W T G T I C P
```

B Guessing Game Write four sentences about when you were a child. Write three *true* sentences and one *false* sentence. Read your sentences to a small group. Your classmates will guess the sentence that is *false*. Use the past tense.

EXAMPLE:

You: I was a good student when I was a child. I played baseball. I learned to read when I was two years old. I loved to dance.

Your classmate: I think the first sentence is not true.

You: No. It is true. I was a good student.

Another classmate: I think the third sentence isn't true.

You: You're right. I didn't learn to read when I was two years old!

C Chant

Starting Over

He rented his house and sold his cars.
He left California and the movie stars.
He found a little dog and named him Jerome.
He taught him Italian and took him to Rome.

He bought a guitar and learned to play.
He sang to his little dog every day.
The dog got homesick. He missed L.A.
He wanted to go back right away.

They got on a plane and flew back home.
They said good-bye to their friends in Rome.
Now they're both as happy as can be.
Back in California, right by the sea.

LESSON

57 Contrast: *BE* and *Do* in Past Tense Yes-No Questions and Answers

Use a past form of *BE*—*was* or *were*—with a noun, an adjective, or a place to ask a question about the past.

Questions				Short Answers
with nouns:	Was	it	holiday?	Yes, it was.
with adjectives:	Were	they	happy?	Yes, they were.
with places:	Were	they	at a restaurant?	No, they weren't.

Use *did* with ALL other verbs to make a question in the past. *Did* is a helping verb.

Questions			Short Answers	
Helping *Verb*	***Subject***	**Base form of *Main Verb***	**Affirmative**	**Negative**
	I		Yes, you did.	No, you didn't.
	you		Yes, I did.	No, I didn't.
	he		Yes, he did.	No, he didn't.
Did	she	dance?	Yes, she did.	No, she didn't.
	it		Yes, it did.	No, it didn't.
	we		Yes, you did.	No, you didn't.
	they		Yes, they did.	No, they didn't.

A Complete the questions on the left with *Was, Were,* or *Did*. Then listen to Sam and complete the correct short answer with *was, wasn't, were, weren't, did,* or *didn't*.

1. ...Was... the New Year's Eve party fun? Yes, it .... No, it ....
2. .... the party at Sam's house? Yes, it .... No, it ....
3. .... Sam home at 2:00 a.m.? Yes, he .... No, he ....
4. .... Sam have dinner there? Yes, he .... No, he ....
5. .... the food good? Yes, it .... No, it ....
6. .... his friends dance? Yes, they .... No, they ....
7. .... they quiet? Yes, they .... No, they ....
8. .... they shake hands at midnight? Yes, they .... No, they ....

B Read the paragraph about Mike and then complete the questions with *Did, Was* or *Were*. Write short answers.

Last Thursday was Thanksgiving. I had a big dinner with my family. The food was delicious. After dinner, I took a walk because I was very full. My sister came with me. We were very tired in the evening. We didn't wash the dishes. We washed the dishes and cleaned the house on Friday. We didn't go to work—we had a great four-day weekend.

1. Was Thanksgiving last Thursday? Yes, it was.
2. .... Mike eat with his family? ....
3. .... the food terrible? ....
4. .... Mike and his sister take a walk? ....
5. .... they tired on Thursday night? ....
6. .... they wash the dishes on Thursday? ....
7. .... Mike clean the house on Friday? ....
8. .... Mike go to work on Friday? ....
9. .... Mike at work on Friday? ....
10. .... Mike's weekend good? ....

C Answer questions about a holiday that you celebrated.

- Complete the questions with *Did, Was* or *Were*.
- Write *true* answers to the questions on the lines.
- Ask a partner the same questions and write his or her answers on a separate piece of paper.

What holiday did you celebrate? ....

1. Did you celebrate with your family? ....
2. .... you busy before the holiday? ....
3. .... you wear special clothes? ....
4. .... you happy? ....
5. .... you eat special food? ....
6. .... the food delicious? ....
7. .... you dance? ....
8. .... you stay home? ....
9. .... you go out? ....
10. .... you tired after the holiday? ....

LESSON

58 Past Tense—Wh Questions and Short Answers

Ask Wh-Questions to get information.

Question Word	Helping Verb	Subject	Base Form of Main Verb		Short Answers
What	did	I	do?		You went shopping.
Where	did	you	go?		To the library.
When	did	he	go?		On Sunday.
Who	did	she	go	with?	Her friend.
What time	did	they	go?		At 7:30.
How	did	they	get	there?	By bus./They walked.
Why	did	it	arrive	late?	Because there was traffic.

A Look at Josh's calendar. Then write question words on the lines. Listen to the tape to check your answers.

FRIDAY
(work all day)
7:00 Dinner at Nicole's
9:00 Movie

SATURDAY
9:00 soccer—Kennedy Field (ride bike)
1:00 Do errands: ATM, shopping, cleaners
8:00 taxi to Gary and Linda's wedding

SUNDAY
11:00 brunch with Mom (Alice's Restaurant)
1:00 Library—study with Nicole
5:00 clean, do laundry

	Wh Questions	Answers
1.	Who did Josh have brunch with?	His mom.
2.	________ did he go to the ATM?	Because he needed money.
3.	________ did he play soccer?	At Kennedy Field.
4.	________ did he have dinner with?	Nicole.
5.	________ did he do on Saturday afternoon?	He did errands.
6.	________ did he go to Gary and Linda's wedding?	At 8:00.
7.	________ did he get there?	By taxi.
8.	________ did he study?	At the library.
9.	________ did he clean his apartment?	On Sunday evening.

B Look again at Josh's calendar. Write Wh questions for the answers.

1. mother/his/and/Josh/eat/did/Where
   Where did Josh and his mother eat? At Alice's restaurant.
2. time/brunch/What/have/did/they
   .... At 11:00.
3. soccer/did/Josh/When/play
   .... On Saturday morning.
4. did/How/Kennedy Field/Josh/to/get
   .... By bike.
5. Who/go/with/to the movies/Josh/did
   .... Nicole.
6. study/Why/he/did
   .... Because he's a student.
7. night/on/go/Friday/Where/he/did
   .... To the movies.

C Work with a partner. Ask each other these questions and give *true* answers.

EXAMPLE: Q: What did you do last weekend? A: I played soccer.

1. What did you do last weekend?
2. What else did you do?
3. Did you go out?
4. (If yes) Where did you go?
5. (If yes) Who did you go with?
6. (If yes) How did you get there?
7. (If yes) When did you get home?
8. (If yes) Did you have fun?
9. What did you do on Sunday?
10. What time did you get up?

D Chant

Where did he go?

Where did he go?
He went to L. A.
How did he go?
He didn't say.
When did he go?
He went last June.
Why did he go?
For his honeymoon!

How was the party?
His party was great.
When did you get there?
We got there at eight.
Who did you go with?
I went with Louise.
What did they serve?
White wine and cheese.

LESSON

59 Contrast: *BE* and *DO* in Past Tense Questions and Answers

Use a past form of *BE*—*was* or *were*—with a noun, an adjective, or a place to ask a question about the past.

	Yes-No Questions and Answers	Wh Questions and Answers
with nouns:	Was she an athlete? Yes, she was.	When was she an athlete? When she was ten.
with adjectives:	Was I cute? Yes, you were.	Why was I cute? Because you were funny.
with places:	Were you at soccer practice? Yes, I was.	Where were you? At soccer practice.
Use *did* with ALL other verbs to make a question in the past. *Did* is a helping verb.		
with verbs:	Did she play soccer? Yes, she did.	When did she play soccer? When she was 12.

A Listen to the questions. Give *true* answers about when you were a child. For questions 1, 2, and 3, circle your answers. For questions 4 and 5, write complete sentences.

pets

When you were a child, ...

1. Yes, I did. No, I didn't. Yes, I was. No, I wasn't.
2. Yes, I did. No, I didn't. Yes, I was. No, I wasn't.
3. Yes, I did. No, I didn't. Yes, I was. No, I wasn't.
4. I ________________________________.
5. I ________________________________.

B Answer the questions. Write complete sentences.

When you were a child ...

1. Were you a good student? ....
2. What did you like to study? ....
3. Was school difficult for you? ....
4. Where was your school? ....
5. Did you play sports at school? ....
6. If yes, what did you play? ....
7. Did you play a musical instrument? ....
8. If yes, what did you play? ....
9. Were you a happy child? ....
10. Why were you happy/unhappy? ....

C Write five questions to ask your classmates about when they were children. Write their first names on the right.

	Questions	Students who said *Yes*	Students who said *No*
	EXAMPLE: Did you ride a bike?	Kim	Katrina
1.	Were you .... ?	....	....
2.	Did you .... ?	....	....
3.	Did you .... ?	....	....
4.	Were you .... ?	....	....
5.	Did you .... ?	....	....

Now write five sentences about your classmates who said *Yes* and five sentences about your classmates who said *No*.

	Yes		No
	EXAMPLE: Kim rode a bike.		Katrina didn't ride a bike.
1.	....	**1.**	....
2.	....	**2.**	....
3.	....	**3.**	....
4.	....	**4.**	....
5.	....	**5.**	....

LESSON 60

Contrast: Three Verb Tenses Present, Present Continuous, and Past

Use the present tense to talk about *every day*.
I study English every day. **She studies English every day.**
Use the present continuous tense to talk about *right now*.
I am studying English right now. **She is studying English right now.**
Use the past tense to talk about *a time before now*.
I studied English last year. **She studied English last year.**

A Read the story about Ricky, a famous movie star. Underline the verbs. Write the verb tense above each verb: 'pres' for the present tense, 'pc' for the present continuous tense, and 'past' for the past tense. Then listen as you read along.

A teenager is a person between 13 and 19 years old.

Thirty years ago, Ricky was (past) a quiet child. He was very shy. He didn't talk in school. He stayed next to his mother all the time.

When Ricky was a teenager, he went to the movies every Saturday. He wanted to be a movie star. He wasn't shy. He performed in school plays. He was very good-looking.

When he was 25, he got married. When he was 29, he got divorced. He has two children, a boy and a girl.

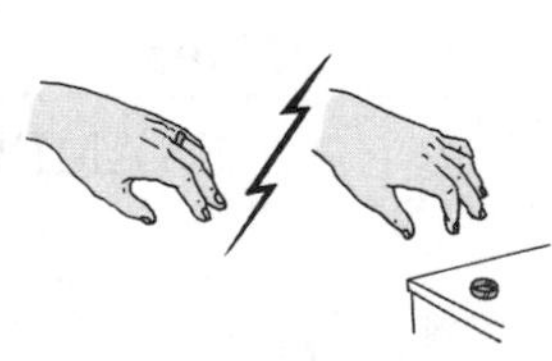

Today he is very famous. He is on TV almost every day. He always smiles and talks to people. He has a beautiful girlfriend, but he doesn't want to get married.

Right now he is flying to New York. He is reading a magazine story about his new movie. He's looking at his picture and he's smiling. He can't believe that he's the boy who was shy and quiet 30 years ago.

B Look at Exercise A. Use the words in the boxes below to write questions about Ricky. Then write the answers. Be careful—only some combinations are possible.

What When Where Why	was did is does	Ricky	doing right now? quiet? get married? get divorced? going? smiling? right now? do when he was a teenager? do every day?

1. What is Ricky doing right now? .... He's flying to New York.
2. ....
3. ....
4. ....
5. ....
6. ....

C Ricky's sister is also famous. She is a singer. Fill in the blanks with verbs in the present continuous, simple present, or simple past tense.

Ricky's sister, Patricia, (be) ......is...... also famous. She (be) .... a singer. She (give) .... concerts all over the world. Every day she (fly) .... to different cities. She (have) .... a lot of money.

Life (be) .... different 30 years ago when she (be) .... a child. She (be) .... poor. She (negative—have) .... money. Her mother and father (work) .... six days a week. She (sleep) .... in a room with Ricky and their two sisters. Patricia (have) .... one pair of shoes and one dress. But she (negative—be) .... hungry. Her parents (have) .... money for food.

When she (be) .... a child, she (be) .... poor. But she (be) .... happy. Her family (love) .... her, and she (love) .... her family.

Right now, Patricia (drive) .... her car in New York. She (go) .... to the airport. She (listen) .... to the radio and she (sing) .... She (be) .... happy—her brother (come) .... to visit her.

Lessons 57–60

Review

BE vs. *Do*
Contrast of Present, Present Continuous, and Past Tenses

A Dictation Two friends are talking about last night. Listen to the conversation and write what you hear. Then practice the conversation with a partner. Key words: *brother, New York, dinner.*

A: Where ....

....

B: ....

....

A: ....

B: ....

B Underline the verbs. Some verbs have two parts. Check (✔) the verb tense for each sentence.

		Present	Present Continuous	Past
1.	What <u>are</u> you <u>doing</u> now?		✔	
2.	We're doing this exercise.			
3.	What did you do last night?			
4.	We didn't do anything.			
5.	Were you sick?			
6.	No, we were tired.			
7.	Are you married?			
8.	No, but I'm looking for a wife.			
9.	Do you want to learn more English?			
10.	Yes, but I don't have time!			

C Complete the questions with *Are you*, *Were you*, *Do you*, or *Did you*.

1. Are you tired today?
2. .... tired last night?
3. .... married?
4. .... have any children?
5. .... do your homework last night?
6. .... working right now?
7. .... like hamburgers?
8. .... at home right now?
9. .... have dinner before you came to class?
10. .... wearing glasses?
11. .... sick yesterday?
12. .... absent from class last week?

D Complete the charts.

STATEMENTS:

Present	Present Continuous	Past
They work hard.		
	He is studying hard.	
It rains in May.		yesterday.

QUESTIONS:

Present	Present Continuous	Past
		Did they work hard?
Does he study hard?		
in May?	Is it raining now?	yesterday?

E Find the mistakes. Rewrite the sentences.

1. When you come here? When did you come here?
2. Where are you live? ....
3. He was worked very hard. ....
4. I don't late for this class. ....
5. I never late for this class. ....
6. Was the class start on time? ....
7. Did he studied English? ....
8. When did you born? ....

LESSONS 57–60

Have Fun

A Unscramble the past tense verbs. Then use the circled letters to make a sentence inside the heart below.

1. J Y O D E E N — E N J O (Y) E D
2. D V S T E I I — V ( ) S _ _ _ _
3. H T B U O G — B (O) ( ) _ _ _
4. L E C A D E N — C (L) _ A _ ( ) _
5. D E V O R — D R ( ) ( ) _

CIRCLED LETTERS: _ _ _ _ _ _ _ _

B **Spelling Bee** Stand in a line. Your teacher will say the base form of a regular or irregular verb. One by one, students will spell the past forms. When students make mistakes, they will sit down. The last student spelling a verb correctly is the winner.

C Chant

She's a very good student.

She's a very good student.
She studies every day.
What is she studying?
She didn't say.

He was a great singer.
He sang with a band.
Where did he sing?
He sang at Disneyland.

He's living in Paris.
He's an excellent cook.
What's he doing now?
He's writing a book.

She was a wonderful teacher.
She taught my sister and me.
What did she teach you?
She taught biology.

LESSON 61

Future Tense with *Be going to*—Affirmative Statements

Use *be going to* to talk about the future.

BE	***Going to***	**Base Form of Main Verb**	
I'm	**going to**	**visit**	**you next weekend.**
You're	**going to**	**see**	**a movie tonight.**
She's/He's	**going to**	**get**	**married in two weeks.**
It's	**going to**	**rain**	**tomorrow.**
We're	**going to**	**eat**	**in a little while.**
They're	**going to**	**be**	**late.**

Future Time Expressions

next week, next month, next year, tomorrow, the day after tomorrow, tonight, in three days, in a little while, on Monday, this weekend

Pronunciation

Going to **is often pronounced as *gonna* or *going ta*.**

Don't write: ~~gonna~~ or ~~going ta~~
Don't say: ~~gonna to~~

A Listen to the answering machine message. Circle the answers to the questions.

1.	Who isn't home?	Barbara.	Ellen.
2.	Who's going to be in New York?	Barbara.	Ellen.
3.	When is she going to be in New York?	Next week.	Next weekend.
4.	Why is she going to be in New York?	For work.	For a job interview.
5.	Where is she going to stay?	At Barbara's.	In a hotel.

B Fill in the blanks with *am / is / are going to* + the verbs in parentheses.

1. Ellen (go) ...is going to go... to New York on Friday.
2. She (have) .... a job interview.
3. Ellen and Barbara (eat) .... in a restaurant on Friday night.
4. They (talk) ....
5. Ellen says, "I (move) .... to New York."
6. Next Saturday, they (visit) .... friends.
7. They (see) .... a movie, too.
8. They (have) .... a good time.
9. Ellen (return) .... to Boston on Sunday morning.
10. Ellen (take) .... the train back to Boston.
11. She (be) .... tired on Sunday night.
12. It (rain) .... on Sunday.

C Ellen is a very busy businesswoman. Look at her calendar. On a separate piece of paper, write ten sentences about what she's going to do this week.

Sunday	11/10	Thursday	11/15
go to the gym		go to the gym	
have brunch with Gary		have lunch with Dad	
go to the theater		practice for my interview	
go to Wendy's potluck			
Monday	**11/12**	**Friday**	**11/16**
go to the gym		take the train to Boston	
go to a computer conference on 58th Street		have my interview!!!	
		go to Barbara's house	
Tuesday	**11/13**	**Saturday**	**11/17**
go to the gym		spend the day with Barbara	
		take Barbara out to dinner	
Wednesday	**11/14**		
go to the gym			
meet with Todd at 10 a.m.			

EXAMPLE: On Sunday, Ellen is going to have brunch with Gary.

LESSON 62

Future Tense with *Be going to*—Negative Statements

Add *not* between a form of *BE* and *going to* to make a negative sentence about the future.

BE + not	*Going to*	Base form of Main Verb	
I'm not	going to	stay	home.
You're not/ You aren't	going to	go	to the beach.
He's-She's not/He-She isn't	going to	swim	in the ocean.
It's not/It isn't	going to	rain	tomorrow.
We're not/We aren't	going to	miss	this chance.
They're not/They aren't	going to	be	here.

A Read the sentences below. Then listen to the weather report about tomorrow. Circle the *true* sentences.

"Highs in the 80s" = "high temperatures in the 80s."
"high" ≠ "low"

1.	It's going to rain tomorrow.	It isn't going to rain tomorrow.
2.	It's going to be cold.	It isn't going to be cold.
3.	It's going to be beautiful.	It isn't going to be beautiful.
4.	It's going to be sunny.	It isn't going to be sunny.
5.	The temperature is going to be in the 80s.	The temperature isn't going to be in the 80s.
6.	It's going to be cloudy.	It isn't going to be cloudy.
7.	It's going to be clear and cool tomorrow evening.	It isn't going to be clear and cool tomorrow evening.
8.	The low temperature is going to be in the 60s.	The low temperature isn't going to be in the 60s.
9.	The reporter is going to stay home tomorrow.	The reporter isn't going to stay home tomorrow.
10.	She and her family are going to go to the beach.	She and her family aren't going to go to the beach.

B Joey and Diana are going to get married. Write sentences about *what they are going to do* on the first line and *what they are not going to do* on the second line.

1. (They/get married on Saturday)

   They are going to get married on Saturday.

   (They/get married on Sunday)

   They aren't going to get married on Sunday.

2. (They/have a big party)

   ....

   (They/have a small party)

   ....

3. (Diana/wear a wedding gown)

   ....

   (She/wear a short dress)

   ....

4. (Joey/wear a tuxedo)

   ....

   (He/wear a suit)

   ....

5. (They/fly to Hawaii)

   ....

   (They/take a boat)

   ....

C Work with a partner. On a separate piece of paper, write three sentences with *be going to* for each picture. Then share your sentences with another pair of students.

a. Write one sentence about the weather. Use *It's*.
b. Write one sentence about what the people are going to do.
c. Write one sentence about what the people aren't going to do.

tomorrow

EXAMPLE: a. It's going to be sunny tomorrow.
b. They're going to go to the beach.
c. They aren't going to stay home.

this weekend

on Saturday

next week

LESSON

63 Future Tense with *Be going to*—Yes-No Questions and Short Answers

Statement:	They	are going to visit friends next Saturday.
Yes-No Question:	Are	they going to visit friends next Saturday?

Questions		**Short Answers**	
BE + Subject	**Going to + Base Form of Main Verb**	**Affirmative (no contraction)**	**Negative**
Am I Are you Is he Is she Are we Are they	going to leave on Sunday?	Yes, you are. Yes, I am. Yes, he is. Yes, she is. Yes, we are. Yes, they are.	No, you're not./No, you aren't. No, I'm not./——— No, he's not./No, he isn't. No, she's not./No, she isn't. No, we're not./No, we aren't. No, they're not./No, they aren't.
Is it	going to rain?	Yes, it is.	Not, it's not./No, it isn't.

A Janet and Paul are going to clean their house next weekend. Read the questions below. Listen to the conversation. Then circle the correct answers.

Questions		
1. Are they going to clean their house next weekend?	(Yes, they are.)	No, they aren't.
2. Are they going to clean it in three days?	Yes, they are.	No, they're not.
3. Are they going to work day and night?	Yes, they are.	No, they aren't.
4. Is Paul going to clean the kitchen?	Yes, he is.	No, he isn't.
5. Is Janet going to clean the living room?	Yes, she is.	No, she's not.
6. Is Nancy going to clean Marty's room?	Yes, she is.	No, she isn't.
7. Is Marty going to clean his room?	Yes, he is.	No, he isn't.
8. Is Paul going to work in the yard?	Yes, he is.	No, he's not.
9. Is everyone going to be tired?	Yes, they are.	No, they aren't.
10. Are Paul's parents going to visit?	Yes, they are.	No, they're not.

B Janet's parents are going to visit. Write questions with *be going to*. Complete the short answers.

1. Are Janet's parents going to visit? Yes, they are .
   (Janet's parents/visit)
2. ______________________? No, __________ .
   (Janet/cook)
3. ______________________? Yes, __________ .
   (Paul/cook)
4. ______________________? No, __________ .
   (they/eat out)
5. ______________________? Yes, __________ .
   (Janet's parents/bring presents)
6. ______________________? Yes, __________ .
   (Nancy/talk to her grandmother)

C Work with a partner. Write questions with *be going to* and short answers about what you see. Use the words in parentheses. Then practice saying the questions and answers.

Janet and Nancy

1. (pick up Nancy's parents)
   Q: ______________________
   A: ______________________

Police Officer

2. (write a ticket)
   Q: ______________________
   A: ______________________

Janet, Nancy, and Janet's parents

3. (tell Paul about the ticket)
   Q: ______________________
   A: ______________________

LESSON 64

Future Tense with *Be going to*— Wh Questions and Short Answers

Statement:		He	is	going to sleep late.
WH- Question:	Why	is	he	going to sleep late?

WH-Questions				**Short Answers**
WH-Word	***BE***	**Subject**	***going to* + Verb**	
What	am	I	going to take?	Presents for my family.
Where	are	you	going to go?	To my native country.
How	is	he/she	going to get there?	By plane.
How long	is	it	going to take?	Twelve hours.
Why	are	we	going to move?	Because we need a new apartment.
When	are	they	going to go?	Next week.
Who	are	they	going to visit?	Their family.
Special question with *do*:				
What	are	you	going to do?	I'm going to relax.

A Listen to the conversation between the English teacher and her students. Match the people with their plans.

	People	**Their Plans**
....	**1.** The teacher	a. is going to look for a job.
....	**2.** Hiro	b. is going to relax, go to the movies, read, and go shopping.
....	**3.** Angela	c. is going to study English at home.
....	**4.** Kim	d. is going to sleep late.

B Read about other students' plans. Then write questions.

Mario is going to move to a new apartment on Sunday because his wife and children are going to come from Mexico. He's going to rent a truck.

1. Q: What is Mario going to do ?
   A: He's going to move to a new apartment.
2. Q: Why ?
   A: Because his wife and children are going to come.
3. Q: What ?
   A: A truck.
4. Q: When ?
   A: On Sunday.

Tatiane and Bruno are going to fly back to France next week because they miss their family.

5. Q: Where ?
   A: They're going to go back to France.
6. Q: Why ?
   A: Because they miss their family.
7. Q: How ?
   A: By plane.
8. Q: Who ?
   A: Their family.

C Write six WH-questions about the future on a separate piece of paper. Ask a classmate your questions and write his or her answers.

EXAMPLE: Q: What are you going to do over vacation?
A: I'm going to relax.

D Chant

What are you going to do?

What are you going to do?
I'm going to call Jill.
We're going to visit her brother, Bill.
Where are you going to see him?
In a coffee bar.
How are you going to go?
We're going to go by car.

When are you going to leave?
We're going to leave at seven.
When are you going to come home?
We're going to come home at eleven.
Have a good time.
What are you going to do?
I'm going to stay home and watch channel two.

Lessons 61–64

Review
Future Tense with *Be going to*

A Dictation A teacher is telling a student that the class is going to have a test. Listen to the conversation and write what you hear. Then practice the conversation with a partner.

Teacher: We're ______________________________ !

Student: ______________________________ ?

Teacher: ______________________________ .

Student: ______________________________ ?

B Complete each sentence with *be going to* + a verb from the box.

take	go	rain	eat	do	be	close	play

1. The students are going to take a test tomorrow.
2. Susan's cold. She ______________ the window.
3. I have a cold. I ______________ some hot soup.
4. My son ______________ soccer after school today.
5. Look at the clouds! I think it ______________ .
6. Linda ______________ her homework soon.
7. Look outside! It ______________ a beautiful day!
8. Goodnight. I ______________ to bed.

C Write three things you are going to do tomorrow. Then write three things you are NOT going to do tomorrow. Start each sentence with *I*.

AFFIRMATIVE

1. I ______________________________ .
2. ______________________________ .
3. ______________________________ .

NEGATIVE

1. ______________________________ .
2. ______________________________ .
3. ______________________________ .

D Look at the calendar. Write the words that go with the dates. Choose words from the box.

in three days	next month	next week	next year
~~tomorrow~~	the day after tomorrow		

1. April 16, 2005 ......tomorrow......
2. April 17, 2005 ....
3. April 18, 2005 ....
4. April 22, 2005 ....
5. May, 2005 ....
6. April 18, 2006 ....

Today is
Saturday, April 15, 2005

E Complete the conversation. Write questions. Use *be going to*.

A: What are you going to do on your vacation?......?

B: I'm going to take a trip.

A: ....?

B: I'm going to go to Los Angeles.

A: ....?

B: I'm going to go with my parents.

A: ....?

B: We're going to stay at my aunt's house.

A: ....?

B: We're going to stay there for two weeks.

A: ....?

B: Because I want to see my cousins.

A: ....?

B: We're going to leave at 6 o'clock tomorrow morning.

A: ....?

B: Yes, I'm going to go to bed early tonight.

LESSONS 61–64

Have Fun

A Crossword Puzzle

Across

5. A: ______ are you going to leave for your trip?
   B: I'm going to leave tomorrow.
6. A: Why are you going to move?
   B: ______ we need a new apartment.
9. Is ______ going to be cold this afternoon?
10. We're going ______ finish this book soon.
11. It's cold today, but it's going to be warm ______ .
12. It's cold this week. It's going to be warm ______ week.
13. She's going to ______ at a hotel.
14. ______ your parents going to visit?

Down

1. Hurry! You're going to ______ late.
2. A: When are you going to see the movie?
   B: We're going to see it ______ at 8:00 p.m.
3. It's usually cold in the winter. It's usually hot in the ______ .
4. The ______ is going to be sunny.
5. A: ______ is he going to live?
   B: He's going to live in New York.
6. A: How is he going to get there?
   B: He's going to get there ______ plane.
7. It's not sunny. It's ______ .
8. I think it's ______ to rain.

B Walk and Talk In the U.S., people often make "New Year's Resolutions." These are promises you make to yourself. Imagine it is New Year's Day. Ask five students "What are your New Year's Resolutions?" Complete the chart.

First Name	New Year's Resolutions
Ellen	I'm going to exercise more. I'm not going to eat candy.
1.	
2.	
3.	
4.	
5.	

C Chant

Future Plans

He's going to go to the mountains,
But he isn't going to ski.

It's going to be a cheap vacation,
But it's not going to be free.

It's going to be cold,
But it isn't going to snow.

His wife has to work,
So she isn't going to go.

He's going to take his banjo,
But he isn't going to play.

He's going to love the mountains,
But he isn't going to stay.

Appendices

Appendix A

Comparison of Verb Tenses—Affirmative & Negative—Regular Verbs

	Present	Present Continuous	Past	Future
I	work don't work	am working am not working	worked didn't work	am going to work am not going to work
She/He/It	works doesn't work	is working isn't working	worked didn't work	is going to work isn't going to work
You/We/They	work don't work	are working aren't working	worked didn't work	are going to work aren't going to work
I	study don't study	am studying am not studying	studied didn't study	am going to study am not going to study
She/He/It	studies doesn't study	is studying isn't studying	studied didn't study	is going to study isn't going to study
You/We/They	study don't study	are studying aren't studying	studied didn't study	are going to study aren't going to study
I	stop don't stop	am stopping am not stopping	stopped didn't stop	am going to stop am not going to stop
She/He/It	stops doesn't stop	is stopping isn't stopping	stopped didn't stop	is going to stop isn't going to stop
You/We/They	stop don't stop	are stopping aren't stopping	stopped didn't stop	are going to stop aren't going to stop
I	watch don't watch	am watching am not watching	watched didn't watch	am going to watch am not going to watch
She/He/It	watches doesn't watch	is watching isn't watching	watched didn't watch	is going to watch isn't going to watch
You/We/They	watch don't watch	are watching aren't watching	watched didn't watch	are going to watch aren't going to watch

Appendix B

Comparison of Verb Tenses—Affirmative & Negative—Be/Have/Do/Go

BE

	Present	Present Continuous	Past	Future
I	am am not		was wasn't	am going to be am not going to be
She/He/It	is isn't		was wasn't	is going to be isn't going to be
You/We/They	are aren't		were weren't	are going to be aren't going to be

HAVE

	Present	Present Continuous	Past	Future
I	have don't have	am having am not having	had didn't have	am going to have am not going to have
She/He/It	has doesn't have	is having isn't having	had didn't have	is going to have isn't going to have
You/We/They	have don't have	are having aren't having	had didn't have	are going to have aren't going to have

DO

	Present	Present Continuous	Past	Future
I	do don't do	am doing am not doing	did didn't do	am going to do am not going to do
She/He/It	does doesn't do	is doing isn't doing	did didn't do	is going to do isn't going to do
You/We/They	do don't do	are doing aren't doing	did didn't do	are going to do aren't going to do

GO

	Present	Present Continuous	Past	Future
I	go don't go	am going am not going	went didn't go	am going to go am not going to go
She/He/It	goes doesn't go	is going isn't going	went didn't go	is going to go isn't going to go
You/We/They	go don't go	are going aren't going	went didn't go	are going to go aren't going to go

Appendix C

Comparison of Question Forms with BE

Present, Past, and Future

	Statement	Yes-No Question	Wh Question
I	I am happy. I was happy. I am going to be happy.	Am I happy? Was I happy? Am I going to be happy?	When am I happy? When was I happy? When am I going to be happy?
She/He/It	He is a teacher. He was a teacher. He is going to be a teacher.	Is he a teacher? Was he a teacher? Is he going to be a teacher?	Why is he a teacher? Why was he a teacher? Why is he going to be a teacher?
You/We/They	They are in the store. They were in the store. They are going to be in the store.	Are they in the store? Were they in the store? Are they going to be in the store?	Where are they? Where were they? Where are they going to be?

* *Use* be *with adjectives, nouns, and places.*

Present Continuous (*BE* + verb + *ing*)

	Statement	Yes-No Question	Wh Question
I	I am eating lunch.	Am I eating lunch?	What am I eating?
She/He/It	She is going.	Is she going?	When is she going?
You/We/They	You are smiling.	Are you smiling?	Why are you smiling?

Appendix D

Irregular Verbs

From this book:

Base Form	Past Form	Base Form	Past Form	Base Form	Past Form
be	was/were	get	got	ring	rang
bring	brought	give	gave	say	said
buy	bought	go	went	sing	sang
come	came	have	had	sit	sat
cut	cut	hear	heard	sleep	slept
do	did	leave	left	speak	spoke
drink	drank	make	made	take	took
drive	drove	put	put	wear	wore
eat	ate	read	read		
fly	flew	ride	rode		

Other common irregular verbs:

Base Form	Past Form	Base Form	Past Form	Base Form	Past Form
begin	began	pay	paid	tell	told
break	broke	run	ran	think	thought
cost	cost	see	saw	understand	understood
find	found	sell	sold	wake up	woke up
forget	forgot	send	sent	win	won
keep	kept	spend	spent	write	wrote
know	knew	stand	stood		
lose	lost	swim	swam		
meet	met	teach	taught		

Appendix E

Memorization Groups

(P = Pronunciation Difference)

No change: cut – cut put – put cost – cost read – read **(P)**	***ought:*** bring – brought buy – bought think – thought BUT: teach – t**a**ught	***ew:*** fly – flew know – knew	***got:*** get – got forget – forgot	***ang:*** ring – rang sing – sang
oke: speak – spoke	***aid:*** say – said	***ent:*** send – sent	***stood:*** stand – stood	***old:*** sell – sold
break – broke wake – woke	pay – paid **(P)**	spend – spent	understand – understood	tell – told

Appendix F

Countries/Nationalities/Languages

(related to Lesson 19)

Countries	Nationalities	Languages
North America		
Canada	Canadian	English/French
Mexico	Mexican	Spanish
the United States	American	English
Central America		
El Salvador	Salvadoran	Spanish
Guatemala	Guatemalan	Spanish
Nicaragua	Nicaraguan	Spanish
Other:		
South America		
Argentina	Argentinean	Spanish
Brazil	Brazilian	Portuguese
Chile	Chilean	Spanish
Peru	Peruvian	Spanish
Other:		
Asia		
Cambodia	Cambodian	Cambodian
China	Chinese	Chinese
Japan	Japanese	Japanese
Korea	Korean	Korean
Laos	Laotian	Laotian
Taiwan	Taiwanese	Chinese
Thailand	Thai	Thai
Vietnam	Vietnamese	Vietnamese
Other:		
Europe		
France	French	French
Germany	German	German
Greece	Greek	Greek
Poland	Polish	Polish
Spain	Spanish	Spanish
the United Kingdom	British	English
Other:		
Africa		
Ethiopia	Ethiopian	Amharic
Kenya	Kenyan	Swahili/Kiswahili and English
Other:		

Communication Gap Instructions for Student A

Have Fun Lessons 9–11, page 38

Exercise A, Part 3

STUDENT A Look at the picture of a living room. Answer Student B's questions with: *Yes, there is. / No, there isn't. / Yes, there are. / No, there aren't.*

Have Fun Lessons 48–51, page 154

Exercise B

STUDENT A Look at the chart. Ask Student B questions. Fill in the answers in the chart. Then, Student B will ask you questions. Look at the chart and answer Student B's questions.

EXAMPLE: A: *What was John F. Kennedy's job?*

Name	Occupation	Year of Birth	Place of Birth
John F. Kennedy	______	______	______
Simon Bolivar	______	______	______
Marie Curie	______	______	______
Frida Kahlo	a painter	1907	Mexico
Mao Tse-tung	a political leader	1893	China
Cleopatra	a queen	200	Egypt

Communication Gap Instructions for Student B

Have Fun Lessons 9–11, page 38

Exercise A, Part 2

STUDENT B Look at the picture of a living room. Answer Student A's questions with: *Yes, there is. / No, there isn't. / Yes, there are. / No, there aren't.*

Have Fun Lessons 48–51, page 154

Exercise B

STUDENT B Look at the chart. Ask Student A questions. Fill in the answers in the chart. Then, Student A will ask you questions. Look at the chart and answer Student A's questions.

EXAMPLE: B: *What was Frida Kahlo's job?*

Name	Occupation	Year of Birth	Place of Birth
John F. Kennedy	an American president	1920	the U.S.
Simon Bolivar	an explorer	1532	Spain
Marie Curie	a scientist	1867	Poland
Frida Kahlo	____________	____________	____________
Mao Tse-tung	____________	____________	____________
Cleopatra	____________	____________	____________

Listening Script

Lesson 1

A

SINGULAR NOUNS:
a clock
a grandfather
a bedroom
a mother
a kitchen
a wife
a living room
a husband
a lamp
a backyard
a house

PLURAL NOUNS:
tables
sofas
windows
chairs

Lesson 3

A

1. happy/sad
2. cold/hot
3. big/little
4. old/young

B

1. expensive/cheap
2. black/white
3. long/short
4. beautiful/ugly

Lesson 4

A

1. eat, cook, wash
2. be, pay, cry
3. read, write, listen
4. teach, study, learn
5. smile, dance, talk

Lesson 6

A

1. They aren't happy.
2. You're not old.
3. He's not tall.
4. It isn't cold.
5. It's blue.
6. She isn't sad.
7. We're not short.
8. I'm young.

Lesson 7

A

1. The jewelry store is expensive. It's an expensive jewelry store.
2. The bookstore is crowded. It's a crowded bookstore.
3. The music store is noisy. It's a noisy music store.
4. The salespeople are friendly. They're friendly salespeople.
5. The children are happy. They're happy children.
6. The restaurant is great. It's a great restaurant.
7. The waitress is young. She's a young waitress.
8. The waiter is old. He's an old waiter.

Lesson 8

A

1. Susan is always early for work.
2. Steve is sometimes late for work. Sometimes Steve is late for work. Steve is late for work sometimes.
3. Susan and Steve are sometimes absent from school. Sometimes Susan and Steve are absent from school. Susan and Steve are absent from school sometimes.
4. Mr. and Mrs. Clay are often busy.
5. Mrs. Clay is never late.
6. The family is often at home.
7. The children are usually busy with school and work.
8. Steve is always at school on Mondays.
9. They are usually late for school.
10. Susan is never home on Saturdays.
11. Steve is always on time for dinner.

Review: Lessons 5–8

A

A: Are you a student?
B: Yes, I am.
A: Are you always busy?
B: Yes, I am.

Lesson 10

A

1. Are you a man?
   Yes, I am.
2. Are you married?
   Yes, I am.
3. Are you an actor?
   No, I'm not.
4. Are you a musician?
   No, I'm not.
5. Are you famous?
   Yes, I am.
6. Are you old?
   No, I'm not.
7. Are you young?
   No, I'm not.
8. Are you middle-aged?
   Yes, I am.
9. Are you a politician?
   Yes, I am.
10. Is your wife Hillary?
    Yes, she is.
11. Are you Bill Clinton?
    Yes, I am.

Listening Script

Review: Lessons 9–11

A

My house is old, but it's nice. There's a big living room and a big kitchen. There are two small bedrooms and one bathroom. There's a small yard with a big tree.

Lesson 12

A

Carmen: This is a great city, Anna.
Anna: Thanks, Carmen. Oh, look—this is the library.
Carmen: It's beautiful. What's the big building over there?
Anna: That's City Hall. And that's a famous park. There are a lot of concerts there in the summer.
Carmen: What's that down the street? Is that a statue?
Anna: No. That's a person! He's a street entertainer.
Carmen: Oh, there's another entertainer across the street! She's good.
Anna: You know, it's noon. I'm hungry. Are you hungry?
Carmen: Yes, a little.
Anna: Well, this is a good restaurant. Millie's food is delicious. Let's have lunch here.

Lesson 13

A

Hi. I'm Ricky. This is my room. This is my bed. That's my closet. Those are my clothes. And those are my shoes. These are my fish. I have three fish. These are my books. Those are my toys near the closet. My mom wants me to clean my room.

Lesson 14

A

1. This is my living room. It's beautiful.
2. That's my stereo. It's very expensive.
3. Those are my CDs. I have 2000!
4. And this is my TV. It's very big.
5. Let's go into the kitchen. This is my favorite room.
6. These are my new chairs. They're comfortable.
7. This is my bedroom. It's very big.
8. That's my brother's bedroom. He lives with me.
9. Look outside. Those are my three cars.
10. And this is my garden. Do you like my house?

Lesson 16

A

Mr. Van Winkle: What's this?
Lydia: It's an MP3 player.
Mr. Van Winkle: What's an MP3 player?
Lydia: It's a machine. It plays music.
Mr. Van Winkle: OK. And what's that?
Lydia: It's a TV.
Mr. Van Winkle: What are those?
Lydia: Over there? Oh, they're computers.
Mr. Van Winkle: And what are these?
Lydia: They're headphones. You use them with an MP3 player. Try them.
Mr. Van Winkle: Hmmm. Very nice!
Lydia: I'll buy an MP3 player for you. It's a present!

Review: Lessons 12–16

A

A: Is this your pen?
B: Yes, it is. Thanks.
A: And are these your keys?
B: No, they're not my keys.

Lesson 17

A

Mary: Look behind you! There are the stars of *San Francisco*!
Tony: What's that?
Mary: You know—it's a TV show!
Tony: Hmm, she's beautiful. What's her name?
Mary: It's Olivia, I think. I'm not sure.
Tony: What's her last name?
Mary: Rivera.
Tony: How about the guy? What's his name?
Mary: It's Tom. And I think his last name is Newman.
Tony: Are they married?
Mary: No, they're not.

Lesson 18

A

1. Molly: Where is my pen?
   Andy: It's on the table, Mom!
2. Molly: Where are my glasses?
   Andy: They're on top of your head!
3. Molly: Where are my keys?
   Andy: They're in your pocket!

Listening Script

4. Molly: And where is my car?
   Andy: It's in the garage!
5. Molly: Where is Katie?
   Andy: She's in her bedroom.
6. Molly: Where is your father?
   Andy: He's at work.

Lesson 20

A

Joan: Hi, Ellen. Hi, Ken. What time is your flight to New York?
Ellen: It's at 11:00 p.m.
Joan: When is your meeting with Mr. Kim, Ellen?
Ellen: It's on Tuesday. When is *your* trip to New York?
Joan: It's in July.
Ken: Hey, what time is our meeting today?
Joan: It's at 2:00. What time is it?
Ken: It's 1:45.
Joan: Oh! Let's go!

Lesson 21

A

Hi Chris,
How is the beach? How is the weather? It's cold and cloudy here. How are your kids? I'm sure they love the beach.
See you on Monday at work.
Have a great time!
Pat

Hi Pat,
The beach is great! The weather is beautiful. It's sunny and warm in the morning and in the afternoon. It's cool at night. The beach isn't crowded and the kids are very happy.
How are you? How is work?
When is your next vacation?
See you soon,
Chris

Review: Lessons 17–21

A

A: What's that?
B: It's a present for my mother.
A: When is her birthday?
B: It's today.

Lesson 23

A

Woman: Hi. Can I help you?
Man: Yes. How much is this lamp?
Woman: It's $12.50.
Man: It's very nice, but it's small. How much are those two big lamps over there?
Woman: They're $15 each.
Man: How old are they?
Woman: Oh, about ten years old.... Hi honey. How old are you?
Little Girl: I'm five.
Woman: And how old is your little brother?
Little Girl: He's one.
Woman: You're a very nice big sister... Sir, I can give you the two big lamps for $25.
Man: How about $20?
Woman: $23?
Man: OK. Here's ten, twenty, one, two, three...

Lesson 24

A

I want to tell you about my English class. Our teacher, Suzanne, is from California. She's always busy.

The students are from many different countries. Nooshi is from Iran and Cai is from Tibet. Angelica and Mario are from Mexico. Chang and Ly are from China, and Benjamin is from Korea.

I like my classmates. Benjamin is a doctor in Korea. He is very funny. Cai is an artist. Angelica and Mario are married. They are both forty years old.

Oh yes, I'm Olga. I'm from Russia.

Lesson 26

D

1. Their day at the zoo is fun.
2. It's sunny there.
3. At the end of the day, they're tired, but they're happy.

Review: Lessons 22–26

A

A: These shoes are beautiful.
B: But they're very expensive.
A: Look over there. Those shoes are on sale.
B: How much are they?
A: They're only $30.

Lesson 27

A

Hi! My name is Angela. I want to tell you about my family.
First, I will tell you about my mother's side of the family.

1. My grandmother's name is Jeanne.
2. My grandfather's name is George.
3. My aunt's name is Rachel.
4. My mother's name is Kathy.

Now I will tell you about my father's side of the family.

5. My grandfather's name is John.
6. My grandmother's name is Sherry.

Listening Script

7. My father's name is Randy.
8. My uncle's name is Ted.

Here is more information about our family.

9. My sister's name is Carmen.
10. My husband's name is Ed.
11. My daughter's name is Linda.
12. My son's name is Joe.
13. My brother's name is Gary. He's married.
14. My sister-in-law's name is Lynn.
15. My nephew's name is Ronnie.
16. My niece's name is Sue.

My children and Gary's children are cousins. Now you know my family!

Lesson 29

A

1. Margaret goes to the store every day.
2. Natasha goes to school at 9:00 every morning.
3. I go to the movies every Friday evening.
4. Deborah and Robin go downtown every Saturday.
5. Chris goes to work at 8:30 a.m. every weekday.
6. Jack goes to bed at 10:00 every night.
7. Sharon and I go to the mall every Saturday.
8. June and Jack go to the park every weekend.
9. We go to San Francisco every week.

Lesson 30

A

Elena and Mario are very busy. In the summer, they go jogging every morning. Every afternoon they go swimming.

Every fall, they go to Los Angeles. Mario's mother lives there. They go to the movies and they go shopping.

In the winter, they go to Canada. Elena's parents live there. They go skiing and ice skating.

In the spring, they go bike-riding every day.

Review: Lessons 27–30

A

1. Every day my daughter goes to school at 8:00 a.m.
2. My husband goes to work at 6:00 a.m.
3. We go bike riding every Saturday.
4. I go to the store on Wednesdays.

Lesson 31

A

Sandy wakes up at 6 o'clock every morning. But she gets up at 6:15. She brushes her teeth and then she takes a shower. After she takes a shower, she eats breakfast. At 7:30, after breakfast, she goes to work.

Lesson 33

A

1. Andy and Sandy have a good time together.
2. They take a walk in the evening.
3. Andy has breakfast around 9:30.
4. He makes the bed every morning.
5. He takes a nap in the afternoon.
6. He makes dinner every evening.
7. He does laundry on Wednesdays.

Review: Lesson 31–34

A

1. Sometimes I'm lazy.
2. I get up late.
3. I don't make my bed.
4. I don't do my laundry.
5. My mother doesn't like that.

Lesson 35

Andy: Oh, hi, Ben! How are you?
Ben: Fine, Andy. Who's this young man?
Andy: This is my grandson, Robbie.
Ben: It's nice to meet you, Robbie.
Robbie: Hi.
Andy: Do you want to take a walk with us, Ben?
Ben: Sure. So, Robbie, do you go to school?
Robbie: Uh-huh. I'm in third grade.
Ben: Third grade! How old are you?
Robbie: I'm eight and a half.
Ben: Really? Eight and a half? Tell me, do you like math?
Robbie: Yes, I do.
Ben: Guess what? I'm a math teacher!
Robbie: Do you teach third grade?
Ben: No, I don't. But my wife does.
Robbie: Does she teach math?
Ben: Yes, she does. She teaches math, English, and science.
Andy: Does she like teaching?
Ben: Yes, she does. And I do, too.

Listening Script

Lesson 36

A

1. Hi. I'm Simona. I love sports, and I always exercise every day.
2. Hello. My name's Jon. I love sports too, but I don't exercise every day. I usually exercise around three times a week.
3. We watch sports on TV a lot. We often watch one or two games every day!
4. I always go jogging in the afternoon.
5. I never go jogging. I like swimming.
6. Jon,that's not true! You sometimes go jogging.
7. I rarely go jogging.
8. Well, we're always busy, that's for sure!

Lesson 37

A

1. Judy and Brian want to invite a lot of people to their wedding.
2. They don't want to have a small party.
3. Brian needs to rent a tuxedo.
4. Judy needs to buy a wedding gown.
5. They like to dance.
6. The wedding is expensive. Judy's parents have to pay a lot of money.

Lesson 38

A

1. Q: What time do you get up in the morning?
   A: Hmmm. I get up at 7:00.

2. Q: What do you eat for breakfast?
   A: I usually eat toast.

3. Q: Who do you live with?
   A: I live with my sister.

4. Q: What time does school start?
   A: It starts at 8:10 and I try to be on time.

5. Q: Does your school have good classes?
   A: Yes, it does. My classes are great.

6. Q: What do you do on weekends?
   A: I'm so busy. I study and work.

7. Q: Do you have free time on weekends?
   A: Yes, a little.

8. Q: When do you do your homework?
   A: I usually do it in the evening.

9. Q: Where do you go to school?
   A: I go to school in my neighborhood. I'm lucky.

10. Q: Why do you go to school?
    A: That's easy. Because I want to be a doctor.

Review: Lessons 35–38

A

A: What do you usually do on weekends?
B: I stay home and sleep.
A: Do you like to go to the movies?
B: Yes. I love to go to the movies!

Lesson 39

A

TV Reporter:
Good evening. Right now I'm at a job fair in the local high school gym. We're inside because it's raining. Many people are getting information about jobs. Let's talk to Pablo.

TV Reporter:
Hi Pablo. What are you doing right now?

Pablo: I'm looking for a job.

TV Reporter:
Are you a student?

Pablo: Yes, I am. I'm studying history in college.

TV Reporter:
Thanks, Pablo. Good luck! Now, here is Paula. Paula, what are you doing here?

Paula: I'm giving information to people about jobs.

TV Reporter:
Well, good luck to you.

TV Reporter:
This place is very noisy! Many people are talking. They are looking at information on the tables. Some men and women are wearing suits. And some people are wearing blue jeans. Everyone is walking around and meeting new people. I'm sure many people will get jobs tonight. But for us, now it's time for a commercial break... We'll be right back...

Lesson 41

A

It's Wednesday night at the Miller house. Mrs. Miller is reading the newspaper. She is drinking a cup of tea. David is working on the computer. Jon and Pam are doing their homework. They are wearing pajamas. Pam is helping Jon with math.

It's Friday night at the Miller house. Mrs. Miller isn't reading

Listening Script

the newspaper, and she isn't drinking a cup of tea. David isn't working on the computer. Mrs. Miller is playing cards with her friends. Jon and Pam aren't doing their homework and they aren't wearing their pajamas. They are watching a movie and eating popcorn with their friends.

Lesson 42

A

1. Right now it's 6:30 in the morning in Seattle.
   Is Jerry waking up?
2. It's 8:30 a.m. in Chicago.
   Is Sue teaching Chinese?
3. It's 9:30 in Miami.
   Are Nick and Alex swimming in the ocean?
4. It's 2:30 in the afternoon in London.
   Is the traffic moving?

Lesson 43

A

Babysitter: Hello.
Emily: Hi, Tracy. How's it going?
Babysitter: Fine. The baby's sleeping.
Emily: That's good. What are the kids doing?
Babysitter: Well, Greg and Mark are watching TV, and Janie is sitting next to me. We're reading a book.
Emily: Oh, that's nice. What are you reading?
Babysitter: Her animal book.
Emily: I'm not surprised. That's her favorite. Can I speak to her?
Babysitter: Sure. Just a sec. Here, Janie. Your mommy's on the phone…
Janie: Hello.
Emily: Hi Janie. Are you having fun?
Janie: No. When are you coming home?
Emily: After the movie. Honey, why are you crying?
Janie: I want my mommy!
Babysitter: Hi. She's OK. She's tired.
Emily: OK. You have my number. Call me if you need me.
Babysitter: Don't worry. Have a great evening.

Review: Lessons 39–43

A

A: What are you doing?
B: I'm making dinner.
A: What are you cooking?
B: I'm cooking chicken and rice.

Lesson 45

A

1. Q: Do you work Maggie?
   A: Yes, I do.
2. Q: Do you wear a uniform?
   A: Yes, I do.
3. Q: Are you single?
   A: No, I'm not.
4. Q: Do you have children?
   A: Yes, I do. I have one daughter.
5. Q: Does your daughter have children?
   A: Yes, she does. She has two boys.
6. Q: Do your grandchildren visit you a lot?
   A: Yes, they do.
7. Q: Are they noisy?
   A: Yes, they are. They're very noisy.
8. Q: Are they visiting you now?
   A: Yes, they are.

Lesson 46

A

We have news for you! A family of Martians is here on earth! They are very friendly and interesting people. This is what we know:

1. They can't drive a car.
2. They can fly and they can walk.
3. They can't swim.
4. The children can play tennis, but they can't play basket-ball.
5. The girl can play the violin.
6. They can't use computers.
7. They can speak many languages, but they can't read or write.
8. Their dog can read.
9. It also can write.
10. They can't fix their spaceship.

Lesson 47

A

This is Harry. He's four months old.

1. Can he walk?
2. Can he talk?
3. Can he smile?
4. Can he read?

This is Gabriela and Howie. They are thirteen years old.

5. Can they play tennis?
6. Can they drive?
7. Can they vote?
8. Can they run?

Review: Lessons 44–47

A

Right now I'm sitting in my classroom. I'm wearing jeans and a sweater because it's cold today. I always wear a sweater in the winter.

Listening Script

Lesson 48

A

1.

Son: Hello.
Mom: Hi, honey. It's Mom. I called you Saturday night, but your cell phone wasn't on.
Son: My friends and I were at a surprise birthday party.
Mom: How was it?
Son: It was great. Our friend was very surprised.

2.

Dad: Hello.
Son: Dad…I have great news! The baby was born an hour ago!
Dad: Is everything OK?
Son: Yeah, Mom and baby are doing fine. But we're tired.

3.

Mom: Hello.
Daughter: Hi Mom! How was your anniversary dinner last night?
Mom: It was fantastic.
Daughter: How was the restaurant?
Mom: Perfect. Your dad and I were very happy.

4.

Jerry: Hello.
Ben: Hi, Jerry. This is Ben.
Jerry: Hi, Ben. How are you?
Ben: Great. How about you? How was New Year's Eve?
Jerry: It wasn't very good.
Ben: Why?
Jerry: Well, first we were in traffic. And the party was very crowded.
Ben: I'm sorry. But Happy New Year!

Lesson 49

A

Interviewer: Hello, everyone. Today I'm talking to Zach Taylor. Zach, welcome to the show.
Zach: Thanks. It's a pleasure to be here.
Interviewer: Can you answer some questions for me about the past?
Zach: Sure. I like to talk about the past.
Interviewer: OK. Here's my first question. Thirty years ago, were you very famous?
Zach: Yes, I was. I played the guitar in a band. I was a good musician.
Interviewer: Were you rich?
Zach: Yes, I was. I had three houses and five cars!
Interviewer: Were you married?
Zach: Yes, I was. My wife was an excellent drummer.
Interviewer: Was she in your band?
Zach: Yes, we were together all the time. We were in Los Angeles.
Interviewer: Were you on TV with your band?
Zach: No, we weren't. But I was on the radio!

Lesson 50

A

Lin: Laura! How are you?
Laura: I'm fine. How are you doing, Lin?
Lin: Fine and busy. You weren't here last week. Where were you?
Laura: In Mexico. I was on vacation.
Lin: Wow! That's great. How was it?
Laura: It was wonderful.
Lin: How long were you there?
Laura: About two weeks. My parents are there.
Lin: Were your children with you?
Laura: Oh, yes. We were all together.
Lin: You're so lucky, Laura. Are you from Mexico?
Laura: Yes, I was born in Mexico City. When is *your* next vacation, Lin?
Lin: In December. I want to go to Taiwan.
Laura: Were you born in Taiwan?
Lin: Yes. My family is there, and I visit them every year.

Lesson 51

A

Ken:

In 1990, I was in Korea. I was single and I was a student. My friends were students, too. We were together all the time. Now I'm in the United States. I'm not single. I'm married. My wife and I are always together. We're both lawyers and we're very busy. But we're with our friends on weekends.

Sally:

A long time ago, my husband and I were rich. We were famous movie stars in Hollywood. Now life is different. We're not married and we're not rich. And we're not famous! I'm in Toronto, and my ex-husband is in Dallas. I'm a restaurant owner and he's a teacher. I'm happy, and he is, too!

Listing Script

Review: Lessons 48-51

A

Last Saturday I was in the city. I was with my friend. We were at a nice restaurant. The food was good, but it wasn't cheap.

Lesson 52

A

1. arrived
2. walked
3. talked
4. cooked
5. watched
6. was

Lesson 53

A

1. rained
2. stayed
3. relaxed
4. stopped
5. walked
6. listened
7. played
8. visited
9. tried

Lesson 55

A

Sunday is my favorite day. Last Sunday I didn't get up early. I slept late. Then I drank coffee and read the paper. I didn't go to school and I didn't go to work.

On the weekdays last week, I was busy. I got up early and went to class. After class I didn't go home. I went to work. When I got home, I did my homework. I didn't watch TV. I didn't go to bed late.

On Friday, I didn't go home after work. I went out to dinner with my friends. We talked a lot, and I got home late. I didn't go to bed early. I went to bed at midnight.

On Saturday, I didn't go out in the morning. I made my bed and did my laundry. I didn't go to school and I didn't go to work. In the afternoon, I went shopping.

Lesson 56

A

Tina:

Last summer, I wasn't here. I traveled, but I wasn't a tourist. I was in my native country. I didn't speak English. I spoke my native language. I didn't go to school and I didn't go to work. I relaxed. I wasn't tired. I had a vacation. I was very happy. But I missed my brother, Thomas. We weren't together. He didn't come with me.

Thomas:

Last summer, I didn't have a vacation. I didn't go to my native country. I was here. But my sister and my parents weren't here. I stayed here and studied English. In the afternoons and evenings, I worked. I was a taxi driver. I didn't have time to go to the beach. I didn't relax. I was very busy, and I was very tired. But I was happy.

Review: Lessons 52–56

A

I was born in Brazil. I arrived in New York ten years ago. I didn't like it here because everything was very expensive, but now I like it here.

Lesson 57

A

Last night was New Year's Eve. I'm tired today because I was at my friend's party until 3:00 a.m. There were about twenty people there, and it was great. We had a delicious dinner, and we talked for hours. We danced a lot, too. At midnight, everyone made a lot of noise. We all shouted "Happy New Year!" and kissed and hugged our friends.

Lesson 58

A

1. Q: Who did Josh have brunch with?
   A: His mom.
2. Q: Why did he go to the ATM?
   A: Because he needed money.
3. Q: Where did he play soccer?
   A: At Kennedy Field.
4. Q: Who did he have dinner with?
   A: Nicole.
5. Q: What did he do on Saturday afternoon?
   A: He did errands.
6. Q: What time did he go to Gary and Linda's wedding?
   A: At 8:00.
7. Q: How did he get there?
   A: By taxi.
8. Q: Where did he study?
   A: At the library.
9. Q: When did he clean his apartment?
   A: On Sunday evening.

Lesson 59

A

When you were a child,

1. Did you like school?
2. Did you have a pet?
3. Were you good?
4. Where were you born?
5. Where did you live?

Listening Script

Review: Lessons 57–60

A

A: Where were you last night? Were you sick?
B: No, I was with my brother. He's visiting me. He lives in New York.
A: What did you do?
B: We had dinner.

Lesson 61

A

This is 555-5986. Please leave a message.

Barbara—Oh, too bad you're not there! It's your sister Ellen. Listen, I'm going to be in New York next weekend! I can't believe it! I'm going to be in the city on Friday for a job interview. Can I stay with you Friday and Saturday night? I really don't want to stay in a hotel. I can't wait to talk to you. We're going to have a great time. Please call me back as soon as you can. See ya.

Lesson 62

A

Good evening, everyone. I have good news for you! It isn't going to rain tomorrow! And it isn't going to be cold. It's going to be beautiful. It's going to be sunny and warm, with highs in the 80s. Tomorrow evening, it isn't going to be cloudy. It's going to be clear and cool, with lows in the 60s. I don't know about you, but I'm not going to stay home tomorrow. My family and I are going to go to the beach! We aren't going to miss this chance to enjoy a beautiful summer day.

Lesson 63

A

Janet: Paul, we're going to clean every room next weekend.
Paul: Can we do it in only two days, Janet?
Janet: Sure we can. We're going to work day and night.
Paul: What are you going to clean?
Janet: I'm going to clean the kitchen and living room. You're going to clean our bedroom and the garage. Nancy's going to clean her room, and Marty's going to clean his room. And everyone is going to work in the yard.
Paul: We're going to be very busy!
Janet: And we're going to be tired. But we're going to have a very clean house when my parents visit!

Lesson 64

A

Teacher: Well, as you know, this is our last class. Tell us what you're going to do during the break. Hiro, what are you going to do?
Hiro: I'm going to sleep late.
Teacher: Why are you going to sleep late?
Hiro: Because I'm tired.
Teacher: I know. I gave you too much homework! And Angela, how about you? What are you going to do?
Angela: I'm going to look for a job.
Teacher: Where are you going to look for a job?
Angela: In my neighborhood.
Teacher: Good luck to you! And Kim, what are you going to do?
Kim: I'm going to study English every day.
Teacher: But school is going to be closed. Where are you going to study English?
Kim: At home.
Teacher: How are you going to study?
Kim: I'm going to do exercises and read. And I'm going to watch TV a lot. And what are YOU going to do?
Teacher: Oh, I'm going to relax. I'm going to read and go to the movies. And I'm going to go shopping. I hope I'm going to see you all when school starts again!

Review: Lessons 61–64

A

Teacher: We're going to finish this book soon!
Student: Are we going to take a test?
Teacher: Yes, I'm going to give a test next week.
Student: Is it going to be easy?

Index